3rd Edition

HOW TO
DIFFERENTIATE
INSTRUCTION

in Academically Diverse Classrooms

3rd Edition

HOW TO
DIFFERENTIATE
INSTRUCTION

in Academically Diverse Classrooms

Carol Ann Tomlinson

ASCD | Alexandria, VA USA

1703 N. Beauregard St. • Alexandria, VA 22311–1714 USA
Phone: 800-933-2723 or 703-578-9600 • Fax: 703-575-5400
Website: www.ascd.org • E-mail: member@ascd.org
Author guidelines: www.ascd.org/write

Deborah S. Delisle, *Executive Director;* Robert D. Clouse, *Managing Director, Digital Content & Publications;* Stefani Roth, *Publisher;* Genny Ostertag, *Director, Content Acquisitions;* Julie Houtz, *Director, Book Editing & Production;* Katie Martin, *Editor;* Lindsey Smith, *Senior Graphic Designer;* Mike Kalyan, *Director, Production Services;* Keith Demmons, *Production Designer;* Kelly Marshall, *Senior Production Specialist*

First edition published 1995 as *How to Differentiate Instruction in Mixed-Ability Classrooms*. Third edition 2017.

PAPERBACK ISBN: 978-1-4166-2330-4   ASCD product #117032   n3/17
PDF E-BOOK ISBN: 978-1-4166-2332-8; see Books in Print for other formats.
Quantity discounts: 10–49, 10%; 50+, 15%; 1,000+, special discounts (e-mail programteam@ascd.org or call 800-933-2723, ext. 5773, or 703-575-5773). For desk copies, go to www.ascd.org/deskcopy.

Library of Congress Cataloging-in-Publication Data

Names: Tomlinson, Carol A., author. | Tomlinson, Carol A. earlier edition.
  How to differentiate instruction in mixed-ability classrooms,
Title: How to differentiate instruction in academically diverse classrooms /
  Carol Ann Tomlinson.
Description: Third edition. | Alexandria, Virginia : ASCD, 2017. | Revised
  edition of: How to differentiate instruction in mixed-ability classrooms /
  Carol Ann Tomlinson. 2nd ed. Alexandria, Va. : Association for Supervision
  and Curriculum Development, c2001. | Includes bibliographical references
  and index.
Identifiers: LCCN 2016049811 (print) | LCCN 2016051073 (ebook) | ISBN
  9781416623304 (pbk.) | ISBN 9781416623328 (PDF) | ISBN 9781416623335 (EPUB)
Subjects: LCSH: Mixed ability grouping in education--United States. |
  Learning ability. | Classroom management--United States.
Classification: LCC LB3061.3 .T65 2017 (print) | LCC LB3061.3 (ebook) | DDC
  371.39/4--dc23
LC record available at https://lccn.loc.gov/2016049811

26 25 24 23 22 21 20 19   3 4 5 6 7 8 9 10 11 12

HOW TO DIFFERENTIATE INSTRUCTION
in Academically Diverse Classrooms

Preface to the Third Edition

Teaching is difficult.

Teaching really well is profoundly difficult.

Even the best among us fall short of our professional aspirations regularly, and feel diminished in those moments.

And yet, for many, the work of teaching is also nourishing. It grows us as we grow the young people in our care. Each success is instructive. Each failure is instructive. We are challenged to become the best version of ourselves as we challenge our students to become their best as well.

One classroom reality that taxes our capacity to teach as we need and want to teach is the great variety of learners who surround us every day. They are mature and immature for their age. They are supported too enthusiastically at home and not supported at all. They are excited by school and terrified by it. They suffer from poverty and from affluence. They are entitled, and they are without hope. They are socially adept and socially inept. They are intrigued, inspired, and shut down by very different topics or issues.

Our students come to us with an array of challenges: physical, cognitive, emotional, and economic. Some have been diagnosed with attention deficit disorder or autism spectrum disorder. About 8 percent of teens have been diagnosed with anxiety disorders (Prentis, 2016), and many more suffer anxiety without a diagnosis. Approximately 62 percent of students with disabilities spend 80 percent or more of the school day in general education classes (Office of Special Education & Rehabilitative Services, 2015). About half of our students qualify for free and reduced-price lunch—a common marker of economic stress (Blad, 2015).

Our students also come to us with highly advanced skills and understandings in one subject, or in many. They may represent a wide array of cultures that vary in significant ways. Many speak other languages more confidently than they speak the language of the classroom. Race is a confounding factor for many learners. Too many students bring with them to school stresses from home that are too great for young shoulders to carry.

Many students, of course, represent several of these realities—a very bright student whose learning disability masks his promise, a second-language learner whose family teeters on the edge of economic viability, a child battered by life and cloaking great academic possibilities that are hidden in equal measure from others and from self.

And at varied points, virtually every learner is weighed down by peer concerns, encounters crippling loss, is distracted by the demands of growing up, struggles with unspoken fears, and feels lost in one way or another. Each of those realities impacts learning—a statement that neither the science nor the common sense of teaching finds worthy of debate. Thus it would seem that to teach well—to teach so that learning enlivens the learner—is to teach with the intent to be attuned to, and to attend to, the variance before us.

Differentiation suggests it is feasible to develop classrooms where the reality of learner variance can be addressed along with curricular realities. Not that it is easy, but that it is feasible—just as it was and continues to be feasible for teachers in one-room schoolhouses, for teachers in multi-grade classrooms, and for teachers in a broad range of more "contemporary" contexts in the United States and internationally who differentiate instruction as a way of life in their classrooms.

The idea is compelling. It challenges us to draw on our best knowledge of teaching and learning. It suggests that there is room for both equity and excellence in our classrooms.

As "right" as the approach we call differentiation seems, it promises no slick and ready solutions. Like most worthy ideas, it is complex. It calls on us to question, change, reflect, and change some more. *How to Differentiate Instruction in Academically Diverse Classrooms* follows this evolutionary route. In the years since the first and second editions, I have had the benefit of accumulating probing questions and practical examples from many educators as well as the continual study of findings from research in both education and neuroscience. This revision reflects an extension and refinement of the elements presented in the earlier versions of the book, based in no small measure on dialogue with other educators.

The title change from the book's initial version, *How to Differentiate Instruction in Mixed-Ability Classrooms*, to its third edition version, *How to Differentiate Instruction in Academically Diverse Classrooms*, also represents an evolution in my thinking and in contemporary classrooms. Demographic changes suggest that we must be deeply engaged with creating classrooms that work well for students whose learning may affected by culture, language, race, and poverty as well as by academic performance. In addition, I have become more and more troubled by our inclination to conclude that a student or group of students is "smart" or "not smart" and to separate and teach them accordingly. While it is doubtless the case that there is a range of learning capacities in any classroom or school, it is equally the case that we are poor judges of the level of possibility that abides in any student. The presumptive "ability" we assign to a student too often becomes a sort of pedagogical predestination. I hope the title change is a reminder to all of us who are educators to teach all comers with the respect, enthusiasm, and optimism that we hunger for our own children to experience in their classrooms.

I am grateful to ASCD for the ongoing opportunity to share reflections and insights fueled by many educators who work daily to ensure a good academic fit for each student who enters their classrooms. These teachers wrestle with standards-driven curriculum, grapple with a predictable shortage of time in the school day, do battle with management issues in a busy classroom, and fight against the test mania that reduces learning to particles of dust. These educators also derive energy from the challenge and insight generated by their students. I continue to be the beneficiary of their frontline work. I hope this small volume represents them well. I hope also that it clarifies and extends what I believe to be an essential discussion about how (not whether) we can attain the ideal of a high-quality public education that exists to maximize the capacity of each learner in our care— each learner who must trust us to direct the course of his or her learning.

Introduction

Bill Bosher, a former Superintendent of Education for Virginia, was fond of saying that the only time there was any such thing as a homogeneous classroom was when he was in the room by himself. He would follow this statement with a longish pause and a questioning brow—then, "and come to think of it, I'm not even sure about *that*."

He's right, of course. All classrooms are heterogeneous on many levels, as are the individual students within them.

Some kindergartners arrive at school already able to read 3rd grade books with comprehension, while their peers grapple for months, if not years, with the idea of left-to-right print progression or the difference between short and long vowel sounds. Some 3rd graders make an independent leap from multiplication to division before any explanation has been offered. Many of these same children, when they reach middle school, make connections between themes in social studies and literature, or apply advanced mathematical tools to solve science problems before other students in their classes have grasped the main idea of a chapter in the textbook. In high school, students who have been seen as "slow" or "average" can surprise everyone by developing a complex and articulate defense of a position related to scientific ethics or economic strategy. Meanwhile, some of their classmates who had always found school a "cinch" find they must now work hard to feel comfortable with ideas at a more abstract level. One student is more successful in math than in English and, within math, more comfortable with geometry than with algebra and, within English, more competent—at least for the time being—with analyzing fiction than with analyzing nonfiction or with grammatical constructions. Another student easily envisions objects moving in space but has great difficulty following the multistep directions necessary to complete science labs.

In life, kids can choose from a variety of clothing to fit their differing sizes, styles, and preferences. With just a few clicks, they can create their own playlists one song at a time, free from earlier generations' obligation to buy an entire album just to hear a favorite song. They can access all kinds of media on demand and on multiple platforms. We understand, without explanation, that these choices make them more comfortable and give expression to their developing personalities.

In school, instruction that is differentiated for students of differing points of entry and varied interests is also more comfortable, engaging, and inviting. Even though students in a classroom may be chronologically the same age, one-size-fits-all instruction will inevitably sag or pinch just as surely as single-size clothing would. Acknowledging that students learn on different timetables, and that they differ widely in their ability to think abstractly or understand complex ideas, is no different than acknowledging that students at any given age aren't all the same height. It is not a statement of worth but of reality.

To operate with the assumption that it is of little significance whether a student understood last year's math, or whether a student loses concentration when forced to sit still for extended periods, or whether a student can read the required textbook, or whether words scramble on a page for a student, or whether a student has already mastered the content in the unit of study that is about to begin is delusional.

To argue that we teach too many students to be expected to know them in a multidimensional way is to reject one of the clearest and most fundamental findings of educational research: that learning is relational.

To say that teachers don't have time to attend to student differences is akin to a physician telling a patient that his case is taking too much time to figure out and should therefore be dismissed.

In truth, most teachers grasp the reality of learner difference early in their careers and quickly begin the process of adapting to it. They use humor differently with one student than another. They move around the classroom while most students are working confidently to answer questions for those who are still uncertain with the content. They ask questions targeted at students' different interests or strengths during class discussions. They offer choices of topics for papers or performance tasks. The question is not whether asking teachers to attend to students' varied learning needs is appropriate or desirable, but rather how school and district leaders can systematically and vigorously support the growth in the direction that virtually all teachers begin as a matter of course and a matter of necessity.

A baseline goal for success in today's schools should be helping teachers create "user-friendly" learning environments in which they become systematically more confident and competent in flexibly adapting pacing, approaches to learning, and channels for expressing learning in response to their students' differing needs—learning environments designed to make room for the students who inhabit them. While the goal for each student in such environments is challenge and maximum growth, teachers will often define challenge and growth differently in response to students' current, diverse interests and starting points.

A goal of this book is to provide a reliable source of guidance for teachers seeking to create learning environments that address the variety typical of academically diverse classrooms. It aims to help these teachers determine what differentiated instruction is, why it is essential for all learners, how to begin to plan for it, and how to become comfortable enough with student differences to make school comfortable for each and every student.

1

What Differentiated Instruction Is—and Isn't

Kids of the same age aren't all alike when it comes to learning any more than they are alike in terms of size, hobbies, personality, or food preferences. Kids do have many things in common, because they are human beings and because they are all young people, but they also have important differences. What we share makes us human, but how we differ makes us individuals. In a classroom with little or no differentiated instruction, only student similarities seem to take center stage. In a differentiated classroom, commonalities are acknowledged and built upon, and student differences also become important elements in teaching and learning.

At its most basic level, differentiating instruction means "shaking up" what goes on in the classroom so that students have multiple options for taking in information, making sense of ideas, and expressing what they learn. In other words, a differentiated classroom provides different avenues to acquiring content, to processing or making sense of ideas, and to developing products so that each student can learn effectively.

In many classrooms, the approach to teaching and learning is more unitary than differentiated. For example, 1st graders may listen to a story and then draw pictures about the beginning, middle, and end of the story. While they may choose to draw different aspects of the elements, they all experience the same content, and they all engage in the same sense-making or processing activity. A kindergarten class may have four centers that all students visit to complete the same activities in a week's time. Fifth graders may all listen to the same explanation about fractions and complete the same homework assignment. Middle school or high school students may sit through a lecture and a video to help them understand a topic in science or history. They will all read the same chapter, complete the same lab or end-of-chapter questions, and take the same quiz—all on the same timetable. Such classrooms are familiar, typical, and largely undifferentiated.

Most teachers (as well as students and parents) have clear mental images of such classrooms. After experiencing undifferentiated instruction over many years, it is often difficult to imagine what a differentiated classroom would look and feel like. How, educators wonder, can we make the shift from "single-size instruction" to differentiated instruction to better meet our students' diverse needs? To answer this question, we first need to clear away some misperceptions.

What Differentiated Instruction Is NOT

Differentiated instruction is NOT "individualized instruction."

Decades ago, in an attempt to honor students' learning differences, educators experimented with what was called "individualized instruction." The idea was to create a different, customized lesson each day for each of the 30-plus students in a single classroom. Given the expectation that each student needed to have a different reading assignment, for example, it didn't take long for teachers to become exhausted. A second flaw in this approach was that in order to "match" each student's precise entry level into the curriculum with each upcoming lesson, instruction needed to be segmented or reduced into skill fragments, thereby making learning largely devoid of meaning and essentially irrelevant to those who were asked to master the curriculum.

While it is true that differentiated instruction can offer multiple avenues to learning, and although it certainly advocates attending to students as individuals, it does not assume a separate assignment for each learner. It also focuses on meaningful learning—on ensuring all students engage with powerful ideas. Differentiation is more reminiscent of a one-room-schoolhouse than of individualization. That model of instruction recognized that the teacher needed to work sometimes with the whole class, sometimes with small groups, and sometimes with individuals. These variations were important both to move each student along in his or her particular understandings and skills and to build a sense of community in the group.

Differentiated instruction is NOT chaotic.

Most teachers remember the recurrent, nightmarish experience from their first year of teaching: losing control of student behavior. A benchmark of teacher development is the point at which the teacher becomes secure and comfortable with managing classroom routines. Fear of returning to uncertainty about "control of student behavior" is a major obstacle for many teachers in establishing a flexible classroom. Here's a surprise, though: teachers who differentiate instruction are quick to point out that, if anything, they now exert more leadership in their classrooms, not less. *And*, student behavior is considerably more focused and productive.

Compared with teachers who offer a single approach to learning, teachers who differentiate instruction have to be more active leaders. Often they must help students understand how differentiation can support greater growth and success for everyone in the class, and then help them develop ground rules for effective work in classroom routines—all while managing and monitoring the multiple activities that are going on. Effectively differentiated classrooms include purposeful student movement and sometimes purposeful student talking, but they are not disorderly or undisciplined. On the contrary, "orderly flexibility" is a defining feature of differentiated classrooms—and of any classroom that prioritizes student thinking. Research tells us that neither "disorderly" environments nor "restrictive" ones support meaningful learning (Darling-Hammond & Bransford, 2007).

Differentiated instruction is NOT just another way to provide homogeneous grouping.

Our memories of undifferentiated classrooms probably include the bluebird, cardinal, and buzzard reading groups. Typically, a buzzard remained a buzzard, and a cardinal was forever a cardinal. Under this system, buzzards nearly always worked with buzzards on skills-focused tasks, while work done by cardinals was typically at "higher levels" of thought. In addition to being predictable, student assignment to groups was virtually always teacher-selected.

A hallmark of an effective differentiated classroom, by contrast, is the use of flexible grouping, which accommodates students who are strong in some areas and weaker in others. For example, a student may be great at interpreting literature but not so strong in spelling, or great with map skills and not as quick to grasp patterns in history, or quick with math word problems but careless with computation. Teachers who use flexible grouping also understand that some students may begin a new task slowly and then launch ahead at remarkable speed, while others will learn steadily but more slowly. They know that sometimes they need to assign students to groups so that assignments are tailored to student need but that in other instances, it makes more sense for students to form their own working groups. They see that some students prefer or benefit from independent work, while others usually fare best in pairs or triads.

In a differentiated classroom, the goal is to have students work consistently with a wide variety of peers and with tasks thoughtfully designed not only to draw on the strengths of all members of a group but also to shore up those students' areas of need. "Fluid" is a good word to describe assignment of students to groups in such a heterogeneous classroom. See the Appendix for more information on flexible grouping.

Differentiated instruction is NOT just "tailoring the same suit of clothes."

Many teachers think they are differentiating instruction when they let students volunteer to answer questions, grade some students a little harder or easier on an assignment in response to the students' perceived ability and effort, or let students read or do homework if they finish a class assignment early. Certainly such modifications reflect a teacher's awareness of differences in student needs and, in that way, the modifications *are* movement in the direction of differentiation. While such approaches play a role in addressing learner variance, they are examples of "micro-differentiation" or "tailoring," and are often just not enough to adequately address significant learning issues.

If the basic assignment itself is far too easy for an advanced learner, having a chance to answer an additional complex question is not an adequate challenge. If information is essential for a struggling learner, allowing him to skip a test question because he never understood the information does nothing to address the student's learning gap. If the information in the basic assignment is simply too complex for a learner until she has the chance to assimilate needed background information or language skills, being "easier on her" when grading her assignment circumvents her need for additional time and support to master foundational content. In sum, trying to stretch a garment that is far too small or attempting to tuck and gather a garment that is far too large is likely to be less effective than getting clothes that are the right fit. Said another way, small adjustments in a lesson may be all that's needed to make the lesson "work" for a student in some instances, but in many others, the mismatch between learner and lesson is too great to be effectively addressed in any way other than re-crafting the lesson itself.

Differentiated instruction is NOT just for outliers.

Certainly students who have identified learning challenges such as autism spectrum disorder, ADHD, intellectual disabilities, visual impairment, and so on are likely to need scaffolding on a fairly regular basis in order to grow academically as they should. Likewise, students who learn rapidly, think deeply, and readily make meaningful connections within or across content areas will need advanced challenges on a regular basis in order to grow as *they* should. And students who are just learning the language spoken in the classroom will typically require support as they seek to master both content and the language in which it is communicated. But in virtually any class on any day, there are students "in the middle" who struggle moderately, or just a little, with varied aspects of what they are seeking to learn.

There are students who know a good bit about a portion of a lesson or unit but struggle with specific steps or content. There are students whose experiences outside the classroom weigh negatively on their ability to concentrate or complete work. There are students who are just about to "take flight" with an idea that has been out of their reach and need encouragement and a boost to ensure their launch is successful. Every student benefits from being on the teacher's radar and from seeing evidence that the teacher understands their development and plans with their success in mind.

What Differentiated Instruction IS

Differentiated instruction IS proactive.

In a differentiated classroom, the teacher assumes that different learners have differing needs and proactively plans lessons that provide a variety of ways to "get at" and express learning. The teacher may still need to fine-tune instruction for some learners, but because the teacher knows the varied learner needs within the classroom and selects learning options accordingly, the chances are greater that these experiences will be an appropriate fit for most learners. Effective differentiation is typically designed to be robust enough to engage and challenge the full range of learners in the classroom. In a one-size-fits-all approach, the teacher must make reactive adjustments whenever it becomes apparent that a lesson is not working for some of the learners for whom it was intended.

For example, many students at all grade levels struggle with reading. Those students need a curriculum with regular, built-in, structured, and supported opportunities to develop the skills of competent readers. While it may be thoughtful, and helpful in the short term, for a teacher to provide both oral and written directions for a task so that students can hear what they might not be able to read with confidence, their fundamental reading problems are unlikely to diminish unless the teacher makes proactive plans to help students acquire the specific reading skills necessary for success in that particular content area.

Differentiated instruction IS more qualitative than quantitative.

Many teachers incorrectly assume that differentiating instruction means giving some students more work to do, and others less. For example, a teacher might assign two book reports to advanced readers and only one to struggling readers. Or a struggling math student might have to complete only computation problems while advanced math students complete the computation problems plus a few word problems.

Although such approaches to differentiation may seem reasonable, they are typically ineffective. One book report may be too demanding for a struggling learner without additional concurrent support in the process of reading as well as interpreting the text. Or a student who is perfectly capable of acting out what happened in the book might be overwhelmed by writing a three-page report. If writing one book report is "too easy" for the advanced reader, doing "twice as much" of the same thing is not only unlikely to remedy that problem but could also seem like punishment. A student who has already demonstrated mastery of one math skill is ready to stop practicing that skill and needs to begin work with a subsequent skill. Simply adjusting the quantity of an assignment will generally be less effective than altering the nature of the assignment to match the actual student needs.

Differentiated instruction IS rooted in assessment.

Teachers who understand that teaching and learning approaches must be a good match for students look for every opportunity to know their students better. They see conversations with individuals, classroom discussions, student work, observation, and formal assessment as ways to keep gaining insight into what works for each learner. What they learn becomes a catalyst for crafting instruction in ways that help every student make the most of his or her potential and talents.

In a differentiated classroom, assessment is no longer predominantly something that happens at the end of a unit to determine "who got it." Diagnostic pre-assessment routinely takes place as a unit begins, to shed light on individuals' particular needs and interests in relation to the unit's goals. Throughout the unit, systematically and in a variety of ways, the teacher assesses students' developing readiness levels, interests, and approaches to learning and then designs learning experiences based on the latest, best understanding of students' needs. Culminating products, or other means of "final" or summative assessment, take many forms, with the goal of finding a way for each student to most successfully share what he or she has learned over the course of the unit.

Differentiated instruction IS taking multiple approaches to content, process, and product.

In all classrooms, teachers deal with at least three curricular elements: (1) **content**—input, what students learn; (2) **process**—how students go about making sense of ideas and information; and (3) **product**—output, or how students demonstrate what they have learned. These elements are dealt with in depth in Chapters 12, 13, and 14.

By differentiating these three elements, teachers offer different approaches to what students learn, how they learn it, and how they demonstrate what they've learned. What the different approaches have in common is that they are crafted to encourage all students' growth with established learning goals and to attend to pacing and other supports necessary to advance the learning of both the class as a whole and individual learners.

Differentiated instruction IS student centered.

Differentiated classrooms operate on the premise that learning experiences are most effective when they are engaging, relevant, and interesting to students. A corollary to that premise is that all students will not always find the same avenues to learning equally engaging, relevant, and interesting. Further, differentiated instruction acknowledges that later knowledge, skill, and understandings must be built on previous knowledge, skill, and understandings—and that not all students possess the same learning foundations at the outset of a given investigation. Teachers who differentiate instruction in academically diverse classrooms seek to provide appropriately challenging learning experiences for all their students. These teachers realize that sometimes a task that lacks challenge for some learners is frustratingly complex to others.

In addition, teachers who differentiate understand the need to help students develop agency as learners. It's easier sometimes, especially in large classrooms, for a teacher to tell students everything rather than guide them to think on their own, accept significant responsibility for learning, and build a sense of pride in what they do. In a differentiated classroom, it's necessary for learners to be active in making and evaluating decisions that benefit their growth. Teaching students to work wisely and share responsibility for classroom success enables a teacher to work with varied groups or individuals for portions of the day because students are self-directing. It also prepares students far better for life now and in the future.

Differentiated instruction IS a blend of whole-class, group, and individual instruction.

There are times in all classrooms when whole-class instruction is an effective and efficient choice. It's useful for establishing common understandings, for example, and provides the opportunity for shared discussion and review that can build a sense of community. As illustrated in Figure 1.1, the pattern of instruction in a differentiated classroom could be represented by mirror images of a wavy line, with students coming together as a whole group to begin a study, moving out to pursue learning in small groups or individually, coming back together to share and make plans for additional investigation, moving out again for more work, coming together again to share or review, and so on.

Figure 1.1 The Flow of Instruction in a Differentiated Classroom

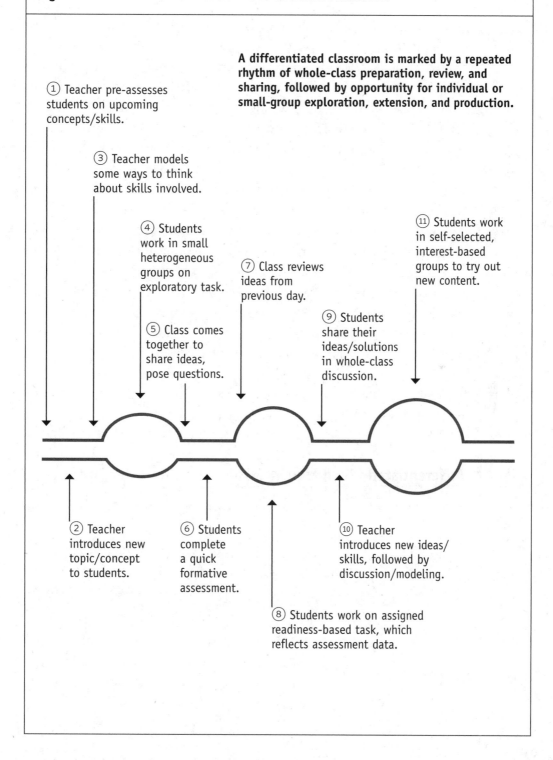

A differentiated classroom is marked by a repeated rhythm of whole-class preparation, review, and sharing, followed by opportunity for individual or small-group exploration, extension, and production.

① Teacher pre-assesses students on upcoming concepts/skills.

③ Teacher models some ways to think about skills involved.

④ Students work in small heterogeneous groups on exploratory task.

⑦ Class reviews ideas from previous day.

⑪ Students work in self-selected, interest-based groups to try out new content.

⑤ Class comes together to share ideas, pose questions.

⑨ Students share their ideas/solutions in whole-class discussion.

② Teacher introduces new topic/concept to students.

⑥ Students complete a quick formative assessment.

⑩ Teacher introduces new ideas/ skills, followed by discussion/modeling.

⑧ Students work on assigned readiness-based task, which reflects assessment data.

Differentiated instruction IS "organic" and dynamic.

In a differentiated classroom, teaching is evolutionary. Students and teachers are learners together. While teachers may know more about the subject matter at hand, they are continuously learning about how their students learn. Ongoing collaboration with students is necessary to refine learning opportunities so they're effective for each student. Teachers monitor the match between learner and learning and make adjustments as warranted. And while teachers are aware that sometimes the learner/learning match is less than ideal, they also understand that they can continually make adjustments. This is an important reason why differentiated instruction often leads to more effective learner/learning matches than the mode of teaching that insists that one assignment serves all learners well.

Further, teachers in a differentiated classroom do not see themselves as someone who "already differentiates instruction." Rather, they are fully aware that every hour of teaching and every day in the classroom can reveal one more way to make the classroom a better environment for its learners. Nor do such teachers see differentiation as "a strategy" or something to do once in a while or when there's extra time. Rather, it is a way of life in the classroom. They do not seek or follow a recipe for differentiation; instead, they combine what they can learn about differentiation from a range of sources with their own professional instincts and knowledge base in order to do whatever it takes to reach each learner.

A Framework to Keep in Mind

As you continue reading about how to differentiate instruction in academically diverse classrooms, keep this framework in mind:

> In a differentiated classroom, the teacher proactively plans and carries out varied approaches to content, process, and product in anticipation of and response to student differences in readiness, interest, and learning needs.

The explanations and examples in this book are presented to help populate this new framework for you as you work to differentiate instruction in your academically diverse classroom. Let's get started with a closer look at the rationale for differentiation.

2

The Rationale for Differentiating Instruction in Academically Diverse Classrooms

Basic as it may seem, the definition of what "a good education" is varies among educators, parents, politicians, and the citizenry at large. Some say a good education is one that ensures that all students learn specified core information and master basic skills according to a prescribed route, timeline, and even script. Others see it as the near opposite: a good education means students pursue what is meaningful to them and on a timeline defined by the students themselves. In between are many other visions—ones emphasizing preparation for 21st century demands, focused on inquiry, advancing a product orientation, built around community service, and so on. Despite our differences in what we believe a good education to be, we all generally agree on the importance of ensuring all students maximize their capacity as learners within that particular framework. Figure 2.1 provides a basic line of logic supporting differentiated instruction.

In a preponderance of schools and classrooms, the unit of focus is the group as a whole. In those places, to differ from the norm in any significant way is to be an inconvenience—a stressor on the system. One of two "solutions" is commonly applied. Either the inconvenient students remain in academically diverse classrooms with minimal instructional adaptations made to address their needs, or they are separated into "homogeneous" classrooms of peers who "learn like they do." In the former case, students who are lost tend to become more so, and students who are advanced or divergent in their

Figure 2.1 The "Why" of Differentiation

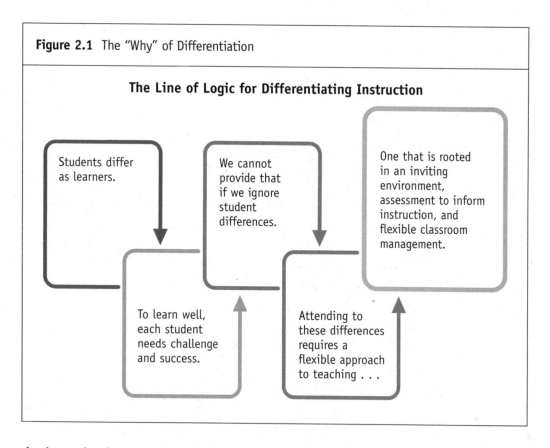

The Line of Logic for Differentiating Instruction

Students differ as learners.

To learn well, each student needs challenge and success.

We cannot provide that if we ignore student differences.

Attending to these differences requires a flexible approach to teaching . . .

One that is rooted in an inviting environment, assessment to inform instruction, and flexible classroom management.

thinking often become more disenchanted with schoolhouse learning. When the latter course is taken, students who are lost typically find themselves taught as though they have little capacity for anything other than *being* lost. In a homogenous classroom, students who are advanced in learning generally receive more experienced and attentive teachers, but too often they find curriculum that is "harder" without being significantly more engaging.

Differentiation proposes an alternative approach—a classroom that honors and adapts to learner variation while building a "team of learners" who work together to benefit outcomes *for* the group and each of its members and *around* curriculum that is designed to be relevant and engaging to young people. Further, differentiation encourages the lifting of ceilings and testing of personal limits and advocates "teaching up," otherwise known as working from a complex curriculum that will challenge advanced learners and providing scaffolding for other students to enable the greatest number possible to access and succeed with the key elements of the complex curriculum and meaning-rich learning experiences.

Considered alongside the more standard approaches to attending to students' varied learning needs, differentiation is far more likely to provide virtually all students equity of access to a high-quality education. This is because it's rooted in our best understanding of how people learn.

How People Learn Best: The Engine That Drives Effective Differentiation

We actually know a great deal about how people learn. For example, we know that each learner must make meaning of what teachers seek to teach. We know that the meaning-making process is influenced by the student's prior understandings, interests, beliefs, how the student learns best, and the student's attitudes about self and school (National Research Council, 1999).

We also know that learning takes place most effectively in classrooms where knowledge is clearly and powerfully organized (Erickson, 2006; National Research Council, 1999; Wiggins & McTighe, 2005), students are highly active in the learning process (Hattie, 2009, 2012; McTighe & Wiggins, 2013; National Research Council, 1999; Sousa, 2011), assessments are rich and varied and yield meaningful feedback (Black & Wiliam, 2010; Hattie, 2009, 2012; National Research Council, 1999), and students feel a sense of safety and community (Hattie, 2009, 2012; National Research Council, 1999).

We know that learning happens best when a learning experience pushes the learner a bit beyond his or her independence level. If the challenge is too little, as when a student continues to work on understandings and skills already mastered, little if any new learning takes place. If the challenge is too great, and tasks are far beyond a student's current point of mastery, the outcome is frustration, not learning (Sousa & Tomlinson, 2011; Vygotsky, 1986; Willis, 2006).

In addition, we know that motivation to learn increases when the learner feels a kinship with, interest in, or passion for the subject (Piaget, 1978; Wolfe, 2010). Further, we know that people go about learning in a wide variety of ways, influenced by how our individual brains are wired, by our culture, and by our gender (Delpit, 1995; Gardner, 1983; Gay, 2013; Ladson-Billings, 1995; Noddings, 2005; Sternberg, 1985; Tannen, 2013).

In the end, we can draw at least three powerful conclusions about teaching and learning:

1. While the image of a "standard issue" student is comfortable, it denies most of what we know about the wide variance that inevitably exists within any group of learners.

2. There is no substitute for highly relevant, meaning-rich, student-focused curriculum and instruction in every classroom.

3. Even in the presence of high-quality curriculum and instruction, we will fall woefully short of the goal of helping each learner build a good life through the power of education unless we consistently seek to understand that learner, understand that learner's progression of growth in critical content and skills, and build bridges between the learner and learning.

These three conclusions are the engine that drives effective differentiation. They, along with our best knowledge of what makes learning happen, are non-negotiables in a classroom where a teacher sets out to awaken all children to the mystery and power of knowing about the world.

Academically diverse classrooms in which teachers are ambiguous about learning goals, exhibit and evoke little passion, cast themselves as the centerpiece of learning, and lack responsiveness to student variance exhibit little understanding of these various learning realities. They lack the foundation of powerful learning, dynamic curriculum and instruction, and the intention to connect each learner's experiences with that curriculum and instruction. Thus, these classrooms operate as though understanding can be achieved through ambiguity and as though fires of inquiry will be ignited in the absence of a flame. They appear to accept as given that all students will learn the same things in the same way over the same time span simply because content—meaningful or not—is laid out before them.

Ensuring clarity about where students should end up as a result of a sequence of learning is fundamental to educational success. Understanding the students we ask to learn is foundational to creating learning opportunities that enliven them. Remembering that we cannot reach the mind we do not engage ought to be a mandate for instructional planning. Offering multiple and varied avenues to learning is a hallmark of the kind of professional quality that denotes expertise. Our students, each of them, are individual reminders that we can never stop attending to either the art or the science of teaching.

The focus of this book is the refinement of high-quality, alluring instruction that we call "differentiation." However, this book also calls for clarity and quality in what we differentiate. It is an exercise in futility to try to meet the needs of learners from a base of low-quality, incoherent curriculum and rote instruction. Such approaches, at best, provide learners with several varieties of gruel that will fall short of nourishing virtually all of them.

Looking at the Classroom Through Many Eyes

Their teacher likes kids, and she likes teaching. She cares about her work. She works hard and is proud of her profession. The kids know that, and they like her for all those things. But the day too often seems long for many of them. Sometimes their teacher knows it. Often she does not.

Rama does not understand English well. No one understands her language either, as far as she can tell. The teacher smiles at her and assigns a classmate to help her. That classmate does not speak her language. The classmate smiles too. Sometimes smiles help. Sometimes they seem like music without sound. In math, she understands more. Numbers carry fewer hidden meanings than words. No one expects her to understand, however, and so no one asks her to share her thinking about the problems. That's OK, she thinks, because if she tried, she wouldn't have the words to talk about her numbers. And yet, she's disappointed.

Santiago wants to read aloud, wants to ask for more books about the people in history, wants to add his questions to the ones the other kids ask in discussions. He doesn't, though. His friends are down on school. *It's not for kids like us*, they say. *Where would grades get you?* they ask. Maybe they're right. He knows he won't go to college or get a big-deal job . . . but he secretly thinks about it. And he wants to know things. But it's hard to ask.

Abby reads her mom's books at home. She reads her dad's newspapers online. She and her friends write and produce a neighborhood play every summer. Lots of people come. In school, she's "learning" 4th grade spelling words. She gets As on the tests. She gets As on everything. Still, she doesn't work hard in school like she does when she's getting the plays ready. This makes her feels dishonest somehow. She makes up stories in her head while she waits for other students to learn. They try hard and don't get As. That makes her feel dishonest, too.

Noah hates reading. He misbehaves sometimes, but it's not that he wants to. He's just tired of seeming stupid in front of everyone. He thinks he sounds like the dumbest kid in the class when he tries to reads aloud. The weird thing is that he understands what the pages are about when somebody else reads them. How can you not be able to read something but still understand it? And how can you be a normal 4th grader and not be able to read?

Livvie knows she doesn't learn like the other kids do. She knows people think she's "slow." She has a special teacher who comes to class to help her or takes her to a special room to learn things. She likes that teacher. She likes her main teacher, too. But she doesn't like the fact that having two teachers makes her feel different. She doesn't like the way her peers look at her when she leaves to go to the special room with the special teacher. She doesn't like that what she studies there seems so different from what everyone else in her "real" class studies. She doesn't like feeling like she's on the outside so much of the time.

Daniel likes coming to school because people there don't yell all the time. Nobody hits at school—or if they do, they get in trouble. There are things to play with at school. His teacher smiles. She says she's glad he's there. He's not sure why. He doesn't do well. He wants to, but it's hard to concentrate. He worries about his mom. He worries about his sister. He forgets to listen. At home, it's hard to do homework. He gets behind. He wonders how he'll ever catch up.

Anthony keeps listening in class for questions that sound like something a person in his house would ask. In the books they read, he keeps looking for language that sounds like his and for people he can relate to. He keeps waiting to see how what they're learning will make a difference in his life. He doesn't mind learning. He just wants to know why. He's restless.

Anna is curious. She asks a lot of questions at home. There are so many things she wants to learn about. (Who invented trees? Why are the Jedi good and the Sith bad? Why do people from different parts of the world have different-colored skin?) These things almost never come up at school.

Their teacher works hard, and she cares about them. They know that. But sometimes—many times—it seems like she thinks they are all the same person. Sometime they feel bad or embarrassed for falling behind, or having a question, or wanting to try things a different way, or being bored. Sometimes they wonder why they have to spend so much time with so many tests. Sometimes it feels like school is like a shoe that's shaped for somebody else's foot.

A good way to begin an exploration of differentiated teaching is to look at the classroom through the eyes of four broad categories of students: advanced learners, learners who struggle, English language learners, and learners "in the middle." These categories, of course, are fluid; students can and do move among them at varied points in their academic careers. Nevertheless, we know that much of a student's experience in the classroom is colored by readiness to learn particular content at a particular time. Accordingly, these categories can help us focus our thinking about the readiness-related needs that academically diverse learners bring with them to school on any given day.

The next chapter will briefly examine needs of students in these four broad categories, looking at ways in which teachers in differentiated classrooms might adjust their practices to meet these needs and teach these students most effectively.

3

Thinking About the Needs of Students in a Differentiated Classroom

There is no great consistency within the categories we create to label human beings. In fact, there is seldom great consistency within a single human being. We are all challenged in some ways and deficient in others. We are all secure and insecure, confident and afraid. We simultaneously seek independence and are dependent. We feel triumphant at one moment and defeated at another. A wholly consistent person would be, at the very least, wooden.

We'd be well served in many ways to simply stop categorizing people —certainly young people whose lives are so plastic and formative. We'd absolutely be wise to shed the kinds of labels frequently applied to students unless we had absolute certainty that applying the label would provide benefits that far outstrip the kinds of negatives that accompany labels. To be clear, the philosophy of differentiation seeks to minimize the application of labels to students. And yet, thinking about instructional needs in broad categories does provide a starting point for thinking about ways in which students might experience school and ways in which teachers might prepare themselves to work with the variety of student needs before them.

In this chapter, we'll look at some suggestions for thinking about the needs of advanced learners, struggling learners, English language learners, and "students in the middle"—and some guidelines for teachers who want to think more deeply and specifically about teaching so that students in these categories find the classroom safe, challenging, supportive, and successful.

As you read, please remember these caveats: few students are advanced in everything all the time, few struggle in everything all the time, few are "typical" of grade or age expectations in every aspect; and if we get it right, English language learners will shed that designation sooner rather than later.

Thinking About and Addressing the Needs of Advanced Learners

Watch your students. Listen to their questions, answers, and conversations. Look at their work. It won't take long to notice that some students have great stores of knowledge or broad background experiences or sophisticated vocabularies or an ability to make connections that surprise you. This kind of information provides a starting point for thinking about students who may already be well ahead of the learning curve you're hoping to establish in a unit of study. Be careful, though: advanced students are not a fixed "batch" of learners, and they aren't always easily spotted.

Some students may be advanced in September and not in May—or in May but not in September. Some may be advanced in math but not in reading, or in lab work but not in memorization of related scientific formulas. Some may be advanced for a short time, while others will be advanced throughout their lives but only in certain endeavors. Some learners are consistently advanced in many areas. Some advanced learners take care to hide their status because they fear peer ramifications for appearing "too smart." Some students are clearly advanced when we see them in the context of the very limited experiences life has offered them, but do not stand out as remarkable if we compare them only to their more privileged peers.

Because the primary intent of differentiated instruction is to maximize student capacity, when you can see (or you have a hunch) that a student can learn more deeply, move at a brisker pace, or make more connections than instructional blueprints might suggest, that's the time to offer them advanced learning opportunities. Advanced learning opportunities offer more complexity and a broader reach of implications than less advanced assignments would generally afford. Note that "advanced assignment" is not a synonym for a "harder" assignment; it's one that provides the degree of intellectual challenge a student needs in order to grow academically.

Advanced learners, like all learners, need help in developing their abilities. It is every bit as damaging in the long term to "under challenge" advanced learners as it is to overlook the frustrations and mounting academic gaps in struggling ones. Without teachers who consistently coach them for growth or curriculum that regularly asks them to stretch, these learners may fail to achieve their potential and suffer a number of related consequences.

First, advanced learners can become mentally lazy, even though they do well in school. We have evidence (Altintas & Ozdemir, 2015; Clark, 1992; Ornstein & Thompson, 1984) that a brain loses capacity and "tone" without vigorous use in much the same way that a little-used muscle does. If a student produces "success" without effort, potential brainpower can be lost.

Under-challenged advanced learners may also fail to develop valuable study and coping skills. Students who coast through school with only modest effort may look successful, but often they get good grades without learning to work hard. We graduate many highly able students who believe, erroneously, that success comes easy, comes quickly, and should be effortless. When they encounter the need to work hard, to study, to grapple with ideas or persist in the face of uncertainty, they become frightened, resentful, or frustrated.

Consider, too, that advanced learners may become hooked on the trappings of success rather than being exhilarated by taking on meaningful challenges. Many of them come to believe that grades are more important than ideas, that praise is more important than taking intellectual risks, and that being right is more valuable than making new discoveries. Unfortunately, many advanced learners quickly learn to do what is "safe" or what "pays" rather than what could result in greater long-term learning.

We praise advanced learners for being the best readers, assign them to help others who don't get the math, and compliment them when they achieve the highest scores on tests. Given how pleased and excited everyone is about their performance, it's understandable that these students want to continue being the best. They tend to attach a great deal of self-worth to the rewards of schooling. Failure becomes something to avoid at all costs. Some advanced learners develop compulsive behaviors, from excessive worry to procrastination to eating disorders, and occasionally even commit suicide. Because creative production typically has a high failure-to-success ratio, many advanced learners simply become less productive and less satisfied. They have tremendous capacity to be producers of new knowledge, but they do not dare take the risk.

Perhaps more damaging still is that under-challenged advanced learners may fail to develop a sense of self-efficacy. Self-esteem is fostered by being told you are important, valued, or successful; self-efficacy, by contrast, comes from stretching yourself to achieve a goal that you first believed was beyond your reach. Although many advanced learners easily achieve a sort of hollow self-esteem, they never develop a sense of self-efficacy. These students often go through life feeling like impostors, fearfully awaiting the inevitable day the world will discover they aren't so capable after all.

In short, advanced learners, like all learners, need learning experiences designed to fit them. When teachers are not sensitive to that need, they may set learning goals for advanced students that are too low or that develop new skills too infrequently. Because these highly capable learners lack sufficient challenge, they may fail to develop the desirable and highly educational balance of running into walls and scaling them. They do not learn that informed effort is the catalyst for their success, that "failures" can inform their effort, and that they are most fully the captains of their own success when they understand and employ the power of "reflective persistence" in their work (Dweck, 2008). Advanced learners share all learners' need for teachers who can help them set high goals, devise plans for reaching those goals, tolerate frustrations and share joys along the way, and sight new horizons after each accomplishment. Here are some key principles to follow.

Challenge advanced students to challenge themselves. Start by continually raising the ceilings of expectations so that advanced learners are competing with their own possibilities rather than with a norm. But when you do, be sure to give the students as much voice as possible in what they learn about and how they go about the learning. Teach them how to aim higher.

Emphasize pride in craftsmanship and the satisfaction of struggle. Berger (2003) calls this establishing an ethic of excellence. Note that these attitudes don't come easily for most students—and certainly not for those who are accustomed to achieving a good level of success with minimal or modest effort. Advanced learners, as others, are much more likely to invest in work they really care about and that they have a voice in developing.

Help students know how to achieve quality. Make clear what would constitute excellence for the advanced learner so that he or she knows, at least in large measure, what to aim for in the work ahead. Provide exemplars of complex and interesting products. Guide students in establishing their own goals for growth.

Raise the support system to match the ceilings of expectations. When tasks are appropriately challenging, you'll find high-end learners need your support and scaffolding to achieve genuine success, just as other learners do. Whenever you "up the ante," increase your guidance and support as well.

Be sure to balance rigor and joy in learning. It's difficult to imagine a talented learner persisting when there is little pleasure in what the learner once found fascinating. It's also difficult to imagine growth toward expertise when there is all pleasure and no rigor.

Be a partner in planning and learning. Work with your advanced students to find their next steps. Don't be concerned if they seem to know more than you do about a topic, or about multiple topics! Remember, your additional life experiences, your trust in their abilities, and your mentoring for growth and quality can help you help them even if your content knowledge in a particular area cannot. Learn from them, and don't be intimidated.

Thinking About and Addressing the Needs of Struggling Learners

Labels are tricky with struggling learners, too. The term "slow learners" often carries with it a negative connotation of being shiftless or lazy, yet many struggling learners work hard and conscientiously—especially when tasks are neither boring (e.g., not a steady diet of skill drills) nor anxiety-producing (e.g., not requiring more than students can deliver even when they work hard). "Slow" seldom indicates incapacity to learn; rather, it reflects the likelihood that a specified time frame allowed for learning will be too narrow for the learner.

Sometimes struggling learners are labeled as "at risk," a term that overlooks the portion of these learners that may well be "at promise." One child's struggle stems from a learning disability, another's home life requires all her energy, another just finds this particular subject to be his nemesis, and another would be perfectly fine in class if not for the stress of persistent bullying that happens outside the classroom.

Further, just like with an advanced learner, the profile of a struggling learner may shift over time, as when a student suddenly becomes an eager reader after trailing the class in decoding and comprehension for some time. Many students whom we perceive to be "slow," "at risk," or "struggling" may actually be quite proficient in talents that schools often treat as secondary, such as leadership among neighborhood peers, storytelling, or building contraptions out of discarded materials.

Nonetheless, many students do struggle with school tasks. They are a diverse group who challenge us to listen deeply, believe unconditionally, and move beyond a follow-the-recipe approach to instruction to shape classrooms that offer many avenues and timetables to understanding.

Here are some principles that can be helpful in ensuring that struggling learners maximize their capacity in school.

Teach with belief in the hidden capacity of each child. Unless teachers assume that the capacity for success exists in all students, even when it is not immediately evident, we will see only deficits and risk falling into the "toxic habit" of labeling students as deficient (Ayres, 2010, p. 152). It's a practice that too often blocks adult investment in and opportunities for the very young people whose futures are most dependent on those things. When teachers believe their students are competent and reliable, they create learning environments that facilitate students' success. When students trust their teachers, they are more likely to take the risks learning entails (Goddard, Tschannen-Moran, & Hoy, 2001).

Teach with a growth mindset. People who operate from a fixed mindset believe that their capacity for success—their talent—is dictated by birth and environment: "You're either smart or you're not." Conversely, people with a growth mindset operate from the belief that our most basic abilities are only a starting point and that dedication to a task and sustained "wise" work can greatly extend those fundamental abilities (Dweck, 2008). While many people, adult and young people alike, fall prey to fixed mindset, it is particularly likely for students who persistently struggle in school to begin to believe that their failure is preordained. Before strugglers with a fixed mindset can shed that orientation in favor of a vastly more promising one, they need (1) teachers who believe in them and communicate that belief to them, (2) consistent engagement with interesting work that is just a bit beyond their current levels of competency, and (3) the support necessary to achieve success with that work.

Look for the struggling learner's positives. Every student does some things well. It's important to find those things, to affirm them in private conversations and before peers, to design tasks that draw on those strengths, and to ensure that the student can use strengths as a means of tackling areas of difficulty. As Sousa (2011) notes, students will fare much better when they believe the teacher is more committed to helping them succeed than to catching them being wrong. Believing in students (even when they have little belief in themselves), teaching from a growth mindset, and building on students' positives are all ways to communicate that you are invested in their success.

Remember that success breeds success. School becomes stultifying when educators spend so much time "remediating" a student's "flaws" that there's no space for enhancing their strengths. Imagine spending all day forced to practice doing something that you're not very good at and don't enjoy. This is the reality for far too many struggling students, and it's no wonder they become demotivated and pull away from school. Be sure your struggling learners spend time every day on tasks that that are both relevant to them and help them see themselves as powerful learners.

Be clear about what students must know, understand, and be able to do (KUD) in order to grow in their grasp of a subject. Teacher uncertainty surrounding these learning targets (the KUDs) will only obscure an already difficult view for struggling students.

Work for learning in-context. In other words, help your struggling student see how the ideas and skills in each lesson connect to their own lives, their families, their neighborhoods, and their futures. Helping them do this presupposes, of course, that we, as teachers, understand our students' lives, neighborhoods, cultures, and families and the connections we can make with them. Often, we have our own work to do in this area.

Pay attention to relevance. It's easy to understand why many struggling learners believe school is not "their place." They don't "do school" well today, and yet teachers keep insisting that persistence will pay off "someday"—often in another grade or level of school, maybe years from now. Dewey (1938) reminds us that if school isn't for today, it will often turn out to be for nothing. He believed this to be true for all learners. Certainly it is so for many struggling learners. A skilled teacher conscientiously works to make each day's explorations compelling for that day.

Go for powerful learning. If struggling learners can't learn everything, make sure they learn the big ideas, key concepts, and governing principles of the subject at hand (Hopfenberg & Levin, 1993; Sousa, 2011). Not only does this approach help struggling learners see the big picture of the topic and subject, but it also helps build a scaffolding of meaning, a requisite framework for future success.

Teach up. Plan first for advanced learners. Then scaffold success for strugglers on those same tasks by encouraging, providing support, guiding planning, specifying success criteria, and so on so that the seemingly unattainable moves within the struggling learners' reach. Set important goals of understanding and application of knowledge and skills for struggling students, then figure out how to build scaffolding leading to student engagement with and success in those goals. Don't dilute the meaningfulness of the work. A steady diet of remediation has seldom made students more than remedial!

Use many avenues to learning. Some students learn best with their ears, some with their eyes, some with touch or movement—many with a combination of inputs. Some are solitary learners, some really need to interact with friends in order to learn. Some students work well by gathering details and constructing a bird's-eye view of what is being studied. Others will not learn unless the bird's-eye view is clear to them before they encounter the details. Teachers who provide students with varied ways to access information, explore ideas, and express learning open the way to success for many more students. If a student has opportunities to hear about an idea, sing about it, build a representation of it, *and* read about it, that student is far more likely to find a way to achieve success.

Be ready to break set. The way we do school doesn't generally work too well for students who struggle. Don't be afraid to challenge conventional wisdom about how we do school. Instead of giving a middle schooler who dreads reading an "easy reader," pass on a book or magazine article that seems highly relevant to his life. Instead of giving a 4th grader who has not yet "caught on to math" another round of worksheets, give her a chance to keep the books for your classroom business. Instead of requiring a 3rd grader who dreads writing to get on with the writing assignment, allow her to tell her story first, then (after thought-provoking guidance) illustrate it, and only then find the words to put on paper. Instead of hoping that a reluctant Spanish I student will become more willing and more proficient in the language through rereading the textbook or rapid-fire in-class questioning, match him with a Spanish-speaking peer who needs help learning English. In short, look for new ways to tap into student interests, and don't be afraid to ask the students to help you generate ideas as well.

See with the eyes of love. Some kids come at the world with their dukes up. Life is a fight for them in part because the belligerence that surrounds them spawns belligerence in them. These kids can be challenging for a teacher to embrace. But behind the tension and combativeness abundant in the world of the angry child, what's lacking is the acceptance and affection he or she disinvites. Perhaps a good definition of a friend is someone who loves us as we are and envisions us as we might be. If so, these students need a teacher who is a friend. The eyes of love reflect both unconditional acceptance and unwavering vision of total potential. They also provide clear and high expectations for student work and behavior. Seeing all students with the eyes of love is not easy, but it is critical.

Let students know that you believe in them, and reinforce legitimate success whenever it happens. A teacher who believes in a student will establish conditions that lead to ever-increasing success, and will be sure to point out that success to the student, and peers, whenever it is genuine and earned.

Thinking About and Addressing the Needs of English Language Learners

As is the case with "advanced students," "struggling students," and any other artificial category we create to distinguish students, English language learners (ELLs) are not a homogeneous group. They, too, may struggle in some domains and excel in others. Some are fluent in their home language, and some have never had the opportunity to develop basic literacy skills in that language. Some have superior support systems at home, and some come from troubled homes. Some live in poverty, and some have family means to provide a comfortable standard of living. Nonetheless, there is something of a common struggle among ELLs who have to make their way in a classroom where the challenge to master content is complicated by the language in which the content is conveyed. Many are also striving simultaneously to honor the culture of their birth and embrace the culture of a new place. It's increasingly important for teachers to understand how to think about cultures other than their own and to teach students how to learn the content they are trying to teach. Unless schools work to develop those and related competencies facultywide, they will fail a rapidly growing segment of the population.

Certainly many of the guidelines for successfully teaching struggling learners apply broadly to teaching ELLs: looking for promise rather than seeing only struggle, teaching with a growth mindset, ensuring that the students engage with powerful learning rather than be relegated to rote learning, helping students engage with curriculum that is relevant to their experiences, teaching up, ensuring goal clarity, and so on. Here are additional strategies that may be more specific to ELLs, although many are useful to a variety of English-proficient students as well.

Work to ensure ELLs feel accepted and valued in the classrooms they come to every day. This means seeing diversity in language and culture as a great resource for teaching and learning, and not as inconvenient or irrelevant. It means being learners of our students' languages, as we expect our students to be learners of English. No, it's not necessary to attain fluency in all the home languages that might be found in one classroom, but we ought to learn some basic words. Certainly it's critical for teachers to pronounce students' names accurately and fluently. Helping students feel accepted and valued also requires working toward a multicultural curriculum throughout the school year, seeking to represent many cultures and cultural contributors in many aspects of the curriculum and to present multiple perspectives on issues including, but not limited to, schooling and learning. Finally, it's about creating a place where students can safely share their cultural perspectives and broaden their sense of the world as they learn from one another—one where all feel safe to make mistakes and where all recognize not just one another's challenges but also one another's growth in addressing those challenges.

Build bridges between students' first languages and English. Doing this means tapping into background knowledge and contexts for topics and skills explored in the classroom as well as drawing on rudimentary knowledge of students' home language. Less obviously, it requires you to be sensitive to your own use of language—to avoid rapid speech and jargon or slang, to use synonyms to communicate meaning, and to be generous with wait time so that ELLs have time to process one idea before being bombarded with the next. It means supporting ELLs in building skills in their home languages. And it often means encouraging ELLs to use their home language to bridge to English. They might, for example, initially write in their first language and then translate to English, or express an idea orally in their first language to clarify their own thinking and then reply in English.

Give ELLs the opportunity to talk. It's through continually using a language that a person really learns it. Accordingly, provide as much time as possible for ELLs to speak English, whether it's to confer with others about ideas, clarify the requirements of a task, or have a peer review a piece of work while it's still in process and provide suggestions for improvement and perhaps support for addressing the suggestions. To that end, it's wise to use many kinds of student groups in your classroom activities, including "buzz groups," Think-Pair-Share, and small groups of students who have the same home language and varying levels of English proficiency.

Use many instructional approaches to enhance opportunities to learn. Strategies to consider include modeling, providing both written and oral directions, offering bilingual summaries and word lists, using cueing questions (letting a student know in advance that you'll be asking him or her a particular question in a while), using games and apps for translating and practicing key vocabulary and skills, incorporating structured or guided note taking, setting up word walls with key academic vocabulary or high-frequency words, aural repetition, using movement and images to reinforce language, using manipulatives, representing meaning in text or discussions in varied ways (e.g., drawing, videos, animations), and teaching in multiple modes. There is no exclusive "ELL strategy" that doesn't have utility for some other students as well, just as there is no exclusive strategy for students who struggle, who are advanced, or *any* student for that matter. What's necessary is that teachers understand their students, be prepared with a broad repertoire of instructional approaches, and use those approaches in ways that support growth for particular students in particular contexts.

Position students for success. This involves clarifying not just the learning goals but the means to these goals, and providing support for that journey as long as support is required. It might mean working regularly with students on how to improve in reading and writing, how to use organizers and other structures to help them learn, how to set goals and monitor their progress toward those goals, how to get help when they are stuck, and so on. It definitely means selecting assessments that are not highly dependent on English but instead offer multiple ways for students to take in, make sense of, and express learning. It means providing personalized feedback and helping the ELL focus on his or her next steps. It's important, too, to be sensitive to the fact that ELLs can experience "low status" in a classroom because of their language or cultural differences. There are many things a teacher can do to "confer status" to these students (Cohen & Lotan, 2014) as they demonstrate noteworthy growth—putting them in positions of leadership within the classroom, for example, and offering assistance for these roles as appropriate. In the end, perhaps the best way to position ELLs for success is to provide each of them with daily, visible evidence that you see, appreciate, and vigorously support them and their continual growth.

Thinking About and Addressing the Needs of "Kids in the Middle"

In her compelling study of adults who had been "wounded by school," Kirsten Olson found that the most devastating wound teachers and schools inflict on students is the wound of underestimation (Olson & Lawrence-Lightfoot, 2009). For many adults in Olson's study, the sense communicated by school was that the individual was "just average," and the message was damaging well into the future.

It's easy to get lost in the great middle. These students "do OK." They don't shine. They don't appear to be in distress. In the classroom world, where it seems there are always 60 hands reaching out to the teacher, surely it must be acceptable to let a few students fall off the radar for a period of time.

And yet, in among these kids who don't seem extraordinary in any way, there are ones who need just a little more help to be able to soar academically. There are ones who need to find their voice but will remain mute without a teacher taking time to ask and to listen. There are ones for whom race disguises possibility in the teacher's eyes and perhaps in their eyes as well. There are ones on the brink of struggle who will cross that line unless they receive additional teacher focus or the help they don't know they need. There are ones who are or have been abused and are defying the odds by showing up at school, but are using energies that could power academic success to keep their "shame" hidden. In the middle is pretty much the whole human condition. And every student in the middle is waiting for someone to signal that he is unique, that she is special, and that there is no achievement that is beyond reach. Teachers have the opportunity (and I would argue, the obligation) to be that someone as often as it is humanly possible to be.

Here are some guidelines for mentoring "kids in the middle" for maximum growth.

Understand that every human being needs to feel unique and important —not better than or worse than—but valuable, irreplaceable. Look at your students carefully. Pay attention to the signals they send about their interests, hopes, and dreams. Use these insights to help them find a sturdier voice—with you, with peers, at home. Take care to ensure that no one falls off your radar for long and that you are not more attentive to a few and less attentive to many.

Teach with a growth mindset. Understand that, with your affirmation, guidance, and stepwise support, every student in the middle should grow markedly and discover possibilities in themselves they had not previously "owned."

Teach productive habits of mind and work. Young people who don't perceive themselves as having much athletic potential don't spend a lot of time working out or attending to performance-boosting diets. Likewise, young people who don't perceive themselves to have a great deal of academic potential don't invest a great deal of time seeking more fruitful ways to read a book or use resources to construct an argument or develop a product that shows real craftsmanship or set long-term goals for education. Teach kids in the middle (and others as well) how to tune in to learning goals, how to ask for help when they need it, how to use feedback to their benefit, how to persist when it's called for, how to look at two sides of an issue, and how to set goals for a more promising outcome. Helping students dream is important, but absent an understanding of how to achieve the dream, it takes on the taunting character of a nightmare.

Teach up. As with strugglers, students in the middle need to escape a "middling" curriculum. They need to be positioned as thinkers, problem solvers, leaders, and idea generators. They need to be connected with issues in the community and in the world that call on them to invest themselves in making improvements. If teachers begin by planning a "high end" lesson and provide scaffolding (in the form of organizers, small-group instruction, aspirational but achievable models of student work, peer partnerships, etc.) to enable students in the middle to access the dynamic learning experiences, many more students will look much smarter—and become much smarter too!

Teach students how to be aspirational. Some children are born into homes where college will follow high school as surely as Friday follows Thursday. Those parents know how to prepare for college, how to apply, and how to save for tuition. They communicate clearly about the positive impacts of an advanced education. Children in these homes are actively college-bound from infancy. While lots of kids in the middle (and strugglers) come to school with this sort of explicit sense of the future, many do not. It's important for teachers to convey to students who aren't academic superstars that they have important and compelling options to consider for their futures. It's equally important to help them see how they can go about planning in those directions. The message is not "You have to go to college or you've failed," but rather "You have exciting and fulfilling choices ahead of you and we can work together to help you move in those directions." Every student, regardless of current achievement, should be able to "try on" different futures, look forward to a promising future, and learn early how to actively explore and plan for that promise.

Differentiating Learning Experiences to Address Students' Varied Entry Points

Differentiated instruction is not simply giving a "normal" assignment to most students and "different" assignments to students who are struggling or advanced. That approach usually creates a pecking order among students, which tends to lead to other troubles. Students assigned a remedial assignment that looks simple to others can take it as a message that they are inferior. Advanced assignments tend to look more interesting to nearly everyone except the advanced learner, who may perceive it as more work. The "different assignment" strategy can backfire in ways that cause both advanced and struggling students to feel different from those who do the "real" assignment.

In a differentiated classroom, a number of things are going on in any given class period. Over time, all students complete assignments—individually and in small groups and as a whole class as well. Sometimes students select their groups and tasks, and sometimes they are assigned. Sometimes the teacher establishes criteria for success, and sometimes students do.

Setting standards for success is often a collaborative process. Teachers design all tasks to be "respectful"—that is, to be equally interesting, equally engaging, and equally focused on the knowledge, understanding, and skills deemed to be most empowering in the content area or segment of learning. Because there are many different things happening, no one assignment defines "normal," and no one "sticks out." The teacher thinks and plans in terms of "multiple avenues to learning" for varied needs rather than in terms of "normal" and "different." "Normal" is each student taking his or her own next steps in growth from a current learning position. The goal of the teacher is coming to understand more and more about students' varied points of development so that learning becomes a better and better match for learners' differing needs.

A Final Thought on Student Needs

In the end, all learners need your energy, your heart, and your mind. They have that in common because they are young humans and you are an important adult in their developing lives. How they need you, however, differs in some important ways. Unless we understand and respond to those differences, we fail many of them.

Some of us are drawn to teach struggling learners, while some are easy advocates for advanced learners. Other teachers have a particular affinity for the sort of "typical" student who matches our image of the 4th or 8th or 11th grader we thought we'd be teaching, or they gravitate to students who seem the most vulnerable. That we have preferences is, again, human. The most effective teachers spend a career cultivating an appreciation of children who are not so easy for them to automatically champion while continuing to draw energy from those with whom they feel a more immediate connection. Differentiation seeks to help all teachers become connoisseurs of each student they teach.

The next chapter looks at the role of the teacher in a differentiated classroom. In the end, it's the teacher's will to know and respond to learners as individuals and the teacher's skill in doing so that determine the degree and quality of differentiation.

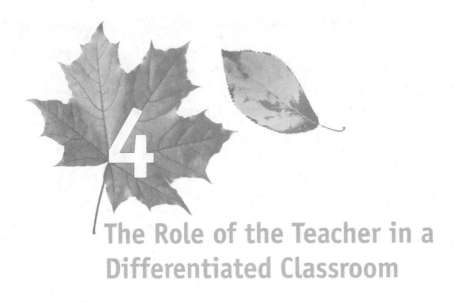

The Role of the Teacher in a Differentiated Classroom

Differentiated instruction in academically diverse classrooms makes good sense for teachers as well as for students. For many teachers, though, before they can offer differentiated instruction, they must first make a paradigm shift.

The Teacher's Role in a Differentiated Classroom

Teachers who have become comfortable with differentiated classrooms would probably say their role differs in some significant ways from that of a teacher in a more "traditional" classroom. When teachers differentiate instruction, they move away from seeing themselves as keepers and dispensers of knowledge and move toward seeing themselves as collaborators with students and *organizers of learning opportunities*. While content knowledge remains important, these teachers focus less on knowing all the answers and more on "reading" and guiding their students. They work persistently to understand their students' cultures, backgrounds, interests, strengths, and needs. Equipped with this insight, they can partner with students to create learning paths that both capture students' attention and lead to enhanced comprehension. Organizing a class for effective activity and exploration becomes a high priority.

Teachers who differentiate instruction focus on their role as *coach or mentor*, give students as much responsibility for learning as they can handle, and consistently teach them to handle a little more. These teachers grow in their ability to (1) assess student readiness through a variety of means, (2) elicit and interpret student clues about interests and learning preferences, (3) create a variety of ways students can interact with information and ideas, (4) develop varied ways students can explore and "own" ideas, and (5) present varied channels through which students can express and expand understandings. "Covering information" takes a back seat to making meaning out of important ideas.

Most of us have not been trained to look at teaching in this light, but we are learners, too. We may not be able to transform our image of ourselves in a flash, but we can and should remake ourselves over the course of a career.

Best Practice Attends to Diverse Learners' Needs

Differentiation calls on a teacher to realize that classrooms must be places where teachers pursue understandings of compelling teaching and learning every day and to remember that no practice is truly best practice unless it works for a particular learner. As Hattie (2009) reminds us, just asking the question "What works?" is a dead end. To keep moving forward, we need to ask three questions: "What works best? Compared to what alternatives? And for whom?"

For instance, most of us who teach know that a lesson that "hooks" students has many merits. Differentiation affirms that principle but also reminds us that what may hook one student might well puzzle, bore, or irritate others. Differentiation doesn't suggest that a teacher can be all things to all individuals all the time. It does, however, mandate that a teacher create a reasonable range of approaches to learning much of the time, so that most students find learning a fit much of the time.

Figure 4.1 offers some key principles of quality teaching practice based on research from three respected sources. As you examine the figure, consider ways in which the elaborations on the principles connect to the principles and goals of differentiation. Making the link between strong teaching practices and differentiation helps set the stage for understanding the role of the teacher in a differentiated classroom.

Figure 4.1 Principles of Effective Teaching

1. The teacher maintains high expectations.

- Sets clearly articulated high expectations for self and students.
- Stresses student responsibility and accountability.
- Sets challenging goals.

2. The teacher creates a positive, invitational learning environment.

- Demonstrates a high level of respect and caring for all students.
- Displays keen interest in and concern about the students' lives outside school.
- Shows concern for students' emotional and physical well-being.
- Exhibits active listening.
- Prevents situations in which a student loses peer respect.
- Knows students' interests both in and out of school.
- Values what students say.
- Interacts in fun, playful manner; jokes when appropriate.
- Maintains a low-anxiety classroom.
- Stresses peer collaboration and cooperation rather than competition.
- Encourages high classroom cohesion.
- Doesn't label students.

3. The teacher engages students in learning.

- Shows joy for the content material.
- Takes pleasure in teaching.
- Links instruction to real-life contexts of the students.

4. The teacher teaches for success.

- Orients the classroom experience toward improvement and growth.
- Focuses on ensuring students have appropriate skills to feel in charge of their learning.
- Creates situations for all students to succeed.
- Incorporates small-group learning with materials and tasks appropriate for the group.
- Uses varied teaching strategies.
- Balances variety and challenge in student activities.

5. The teacher engages in reflective practice.

- Possesses a positive attitude about life and teaching.
- Sets high expectations for personal classroom performance.
- Knows areas of personal strengths and weaknesses.
- Uses reflection to improve teaching.
- Demonstrates high efficacy.

Sources: Brandt, 1998; Hattie, 2009, 2012; Stronge, 2007.

Learning to Lead a Differentiated Classroom

Few of us as teachers automatically know how to lead a classroom that responds to the daunting reality of learner variance. It is a learned skill, in the same sense as any other art or craft. Perhaps a good place to begin is by listing some key skills that a teacher will develop over time as he or she consciously and reflectively works on differentiating instruction. Teachers who become comfortable and competent with differentiation almost inevitably develop the ability to

- Lead students to think about and contribute to the establishment of a classroom that works well for everyone in it.
- Organize and focus curriculum on information, understandings, and skills that are critical to student engagement with content, to their continuing investment in learning, and to a fulfilling life.
- See students as individuals as well as part of the class as a whole and consider needs in both contexts.
- Peel back first impressions, look beyond actions, and push back against stereotypes.
- Give students a voice in as many aspects of their learning as possible.
- Think about instructional time and use it flexibly.
- Find a wide range of materials to help students connect with important ideas and skills.
- Think of multiple ways to help students explore ideas and skills, make sense of those ideas and skills, and express what they have learned.
- Balance attention to group and individual needs.
- Diagnose individual student needs and craft learning experiences in response to diagnoses.
- Provide students with useful feedback that increases their engagement in learning and helps them move forward with increasing competence and confidence.
- Keep track of student proximity to and growth toward personal and group goals.
- Share responsibility for teaching and learning with students and ensure students are prepared for this responsibility.
- Move students through varied work arrangements that allow them to express different aspects of themselves and see themselves and their peers in new and promising ways.

• Organize learning materials and space so that students can readily access what they need without disturbing the work of their peers and without asking for teacher assistance.

• Anticipate potential problems in activities and tasks and troubleshoot them effectively.

• Give thorough and thoughtful directions.

• Teach for success.

Here are three simple metaphors for the role of the teacher in a differentiated classroom.

The Teacher as Director of the Orchestra

The director of the orchestra knows music intimately, can interpret it elegantly, and can pull together a group of people who play different instruments and may not know each other well to achieve a powerful common end. There's a time in rehearsals for individual practice, a time for sectional practice, and a time for the whole group to work together. There's a need to polish the performance of each individual musician to ensure the quality of the work as a whole. In the end, each musician contributes to a meaningful performance and earns the applause of the audience. The director of the orchestra guides, supports, and brings out the performance, but it's the musicians, not the director, who really make the music.

The Teacher as Coach

A good coach has clear goals for the team, and for every individual on the team. Practices involve some common activities, but they will also likely call on each player to improve areas of weakness and polish areas of strength. The coach is generally part psychologist, required to understand what motivates each player and use that understanding to develop his or her skill, by investing sweat and effort and risking pain. However, the coach must also build a team spirit that transcends individual concerns. During practices and games, the coach maintains an active role—running the sidelines, motivating, giving directions, calling small groups aside at key times for strategy adjustments. But it's the team, not the coach, who actually plays the game.

The Teacher as Jazz Musician

Improvisation combines with a high level of musical competence to enable the jazz musician to think both inside and outside the box. The jazz musician keeps the big picture in mind but can add new notes, change tempo, step back so a soloist can assume the spotlight, or become the soloist in the spotlight. A piece becomes longer or shorter, more plaintive or more playful, as the mood of the group dictates. The jazz musician might use call and response to engage others in a dialogue of sound. The artistry and confidence of the jazz musician—knowledge of each song, the instrument, its techniques, and the others in the group—means it's possible to abandon the written score, as needed, for the sake of the music, the other players, and the audience. A good differentiated classroom is a great deal like jazz.

Differentiating Instruction: The Rules of Thumb

Before looking at specific ways to modify content, process, and product for students in your academically diverse classroom, it helps to understand several general guidelines that make differentiation possible.

Know that highly effective teachers teach students first, then content. Students have to know that their teachers see them, value them, and are active supporters of their success. Most students need to feel cared about before they will care about academics. For most students, that means the teacher takes time to learn about them and understand them—and sees *them* before their grades or their test scores. For some students, "feeling seen" can be even more basic than that. Consider one student whose behavior was so challenging that she was bounced from teacher to teacher. About the fourth time she was reassigned, her new teacher sat on the floor beside her and asked a simple question: "What can I do for you?" The girl broke into tears. "I just want a bath and to look like everyone else," she sobbed. Given a chance to take showers, access to clean clothes, and a new haircut, this student's attitude and behavior shifted remarkably (Hayman, 2016). Remember that learning takes place only when fundamental safety, physical, and social needs are met. Caring teachers in all classrooms—and certainly in differentiated ones—know that their success and that of their students is dependent on understanding and working to meet those needs, both before and during instruction.

Be clear on the key concepts, generalizations, principles, or big ideas that give meaning and structure to the topic, curriculum, unit, lesson, or inquiry you are planning. The brain is not designed to amass and recall myriad bits of data on multiple topics, let alone organize and use all that data (Sousa, 2011). All learners would likely fare better if lessons focused on key ideas, meanings, and "stories" that connect with students' experiences. When the curriculum "covers" 500 pages or eons of time or dozens of dismembered bits of information and skills, it is difficult to do much more than drag everyone across the surface of learning in the time available. On the other hand, focusing on key concepts and understandings or big ideas and essential questions can ensure that all learners gain powerful understandings that serve as building blocks for meaning and access to other knowledge. Understandings, or big ideas, act as springboards to help all learners make connections between the topic under consideration and expanded studies, and to understand what they learn rather than simply trying to retain facts. And these learners are more likely to find their school experiences relatable, memorable, useful, and engaging. In schools where there is an agreed-upon curriculum (currently, most schools), it's important to begin planning with knowledge, understandings, and skills you want individuals and the group to have mastered when concluding a segment of learning (for example, K–12 science, 5th grade science, a unit on regional geology), then take a step-by-step journey "backward" to figure out the best progression you and the students can take in order to reach the destination. This model of differentiation refers to the key elements of curriculum as KUDs—**K**nowledge, **U**nderstandings, and **D**o's (skills). KUDs derive from two key sources: (1) required content standards, goals, or outcomes, and (2) the nature and purpose of the content or disciplines being explored. It's KUDs that provide the focus for assessment and instruction.

Think of assessment as a road map for your thinking and planning. Too often, assessment is cast as a synonym for test. We've become increasingly aware, however, that everything a student does, from an oral contribution in a discussion to a homework assignment to completion of an interest checklist, can be a form of assessment. When we begin to see the wide array of assessment opportunities in the classroom, we open our eyes to new ways to learn about learners. Too often, assessment is something that happens at the end of a unit as the way to find out who "got it" and who didn't. Yet we're seeing that assessment that comes at the outset of the unit, or at various points along the way in a unit, will reveal new routes to student success. At those points, assessment invites us to adjust our teaching based on current information and should invite students to examine their current strengths and needs, and to plan for next steps in growth. Too often, assessment is dependent on reading and writing. While those are essential skills for carrying out many roles in life, they are not always the best way to find out what all learners have come to understand and be able to do as the result of a learning sequence. Fruitful assessment often asks, "What is an array of ways I can offer students to demonstrate their knowledge, understanding, and skills?" In that way, assessment becomes a part of teaching for success and a way to extend learning rather than merely measure it. Both formative and summative assessments can be differentiated in a variety of ways, but unless a student has an Individualized Educational Program (IEP) or other approved alternative curricular plan, what the assessment measures (KUDs) should not be differentiated—at least in the majority of schools that work from agreed-upon content standards.

Create lessons that engage all students in critical and creative thinking. In the imperfect world of teaching, you may not always accomplish this as often as you like, but it should be your clear goal. Said another way, it is not acceptable for remedial students to do "low-level" tasks that require only memorization of information and minimal comprehension. All tasks should require that all students, at the very least, understand and be able to apply the meaning of the ideas at hand. Much of the time, all students should be called on to use what they learn to solve knotty problems that defy a recipe-like answer, even though some will need to go about the task in a different way. Some students may need more scaffolding than others to make and support an argument, for example. Some may benefit from using more advanced resources as they construct their argument. Some may profit from a mini-lesson that recaps how to make and support a solid argument. Some may need to develop their arguments orally and have their work written by a peer or adult. Some may need to use materials in a language other than English, or write initially in a first language and then translate into English. But if we acknowledge that argumentation is a valuable skill, we must commit to helping all students master it by providing the appropriate scaffolding.

Design lessons to be engaging for all students. Although drill and practice are sometimes necessary, it is not acceptable for struggling learners to spend most of their time trying to master basic information while other students get to use it. In fact, we now know that many learners who struggle would find learning more natural and sensible if they were consistently presented with problems, issues, dilemmas, and unknowns that require them to use more of what they have learned and are trying to learn (Means, Chelemer, & Knapp, 1991; Sousa, 2011; Watanabe, 2012; Willis, 2006).

Balance student-selected and teacher-assigned tasks and working arrangements. Although the split will vary somewhat for each student, based on the student's maturity, the nature of the task, classroom conditions, and so on, all students should regularly have choices to make, and all students should regularly be matched with tasks compatible with their needs and interests. The goal holds steady: to help all students increase their capacity to make choices that benefit their learning and development as people.

The next chapter provides an overview of learning environments most likely to be hospitable to a philosophy of differentiation.

5

The Learning Environment in a Differentiated Classroom

The tone of any classroom greatly affects those who inhabit it and the learning that takes place there. In a setting that strives for differentiation, the classroom environment is, if anything, even more of a factor in shaping student success. A differentiated classroom supports, and is supported by, an evolving community of learners. What that means is that the teacher leads students in developing the sorts of attitudes, beliefs, and practices that you would find in a really good neighborhood—one that sees to the needs of each of its members.

Characteristics of an Effective Learning Community

Let's look at the traits that characterize an effective community of learners.

Everyone feels welcome and contributes to everyone *else* feeling welcome. Many things make students feel welcome. Certainly the direct and positive attention of the teacher is welcoming. Peers who acknowledge their classmates in positive ways is a foundational expectation. A room that contains student work and other artifacts that are student-designed and interesting to look at and think about is inviting. Flexible and comfortable seating options provide a kind of welcome as well. A time in the day or class period when students and teacher can talk about the day, or life in general, builds bridges between learning and the world of the learner.

Feeling welcome means being in a place where you feel you belong, and where others think you belong too. It also means that key people are making an enduring and sustained effort to get to know you, understand you, and appreciate you.

Mutual respect is a non-negotiable. It will never be the case that we like everyone with whom we spend time. On the other hand, the classroom is a better place when we realize that everyone in it shares a need for acceptance, respect, security, contribution, and success. It is a powerful life lesson that regardless of age, gender, culture, speed of learning, language, dress, and personality, we all feel pain, joy, doubt, triumph—the human emotions. All lives are made better when they are treated as valuable and worthy of respect.

In a differentiated classroom, the teacher helps students distinguish between feelings about something someone did and the value of that person. Further, the teacher helps students learn to solve problems in constructive ways that attend to the issue at hand without making a person or group feel smaller. Respect is cultivated; it requires effort. The teacher is inevitably the catalyst for that effort. It's important to remember that positive humor plays a central role in a welcoming and respectful classroom. Sarcasm and sharp words are virtually always counterproductive and destructive.

Students feel safe in the classroom. Not only does safety presuppose the absence of physical danger, it requires the absence of emotional danger as well. Students in a differentiated classroom should know it's a good thing to ask for help when it's needed, that it's fine to say you don't know, that an earnest question will get an earnest response, that eyes will not roll when someone expresses a thought that seems unusual or evident, that fledgling ideas will be given a chance to develop, and so on. Safety means that when I try a new skill, expend effort, or take a risk with a creative idea, I won't be thought of as foolish or odd. Safety happens when you feel accepted as you are and valued enough that people want to help you become even better.

There is a pervasive expectation of growth. The goal in a differentiated classroom is to help every learner grow as much as he or she can in both general capacities and specific talents. The teacher gets excited about evidence of growth in each individual learner, and in the class as a whole, and expresses that excitement to students. Students learn to chart their own growth and to talk about both their learning goals and ways of achieving them. All growth is worthy of note. One student's growth may mean that the concept of fractions is finally beginning to make sense, while another's growth may reflect an insight about connections between fractions, decimals, and subtraction. In a differentiated classroom, the growth of each of the students is a matter of celebration, and one person's growth is not more or less valuable than another's.

The teacher teaches for success. Sometimes school is characterized by a sort of "gotcha" teaching, in which the game seems to be seeing if the teacher can ask a question or design a test item that will trip up students. In a differentiated classroom, it's the teacher's goal to figure out where a student is in relation to key learning goals and then provide learning experiences that will push the learner a little further and faster than is comfortable. The teacher coaches for student effort and productive learning choices, and will ensure that there is support necessary to assist the student in reaching the goal that seemed a bit out of reach. That kind of assistance is often called "scaffolding." Figure 5.1 (see page 46) lists some common kinds of scaffolding in classrooms. Scaffolding is whatever kind of assistance is needed for any student to move from current proficiencies to the next level of competence. In a good differentiated classroom, the teacher is constantly raising the stakes for success for any individual, then doing whatever is necessary to help the student succeed in taking his or her next step. Remember that everyone's next step will not be identical, and that every student needs scaffolding in order to stretch.

A new sort of fairness is evident. We often define fair in a classroom as treating everyone alike. In a differentiated classroom, fairness is redefined. In this sort of environment, fair means trying to make sure each student gets what he or she needs in order to grow and ultimately succeed. Students and teacher alike are part of the team trying to ensure that the classroom works well for everyone in the class. Regular opportunities for peer conversation, collaboration, and support help students learn to both accept and provide assistance in productive ways.

The teacher and students collaborate for mutual growth and success. In a differentiated classroom, just as in a large family, everyone has to take extra responsibility both for their own well-being and for the well-being of others. In this sort of setting, while the teacher is clearly the leader of the group, students help develop routines for the classroom, make major contributions toward solving problems and refining routines, help one another, keep track

Figure 5.1 Examples of Scaffolding: Ways to Support Student Success
with Challenging Tasks

Clear criteria for success

Directions provided one step at a time

Directions that provide more detail and structure

Directions written in simpler/more straightforward wording

Enlarged type and additional white space in directions or text

Exemplars of past student work slightly beyond a current student's performance level

Frequent check-ins

Front-loaded vocabulary

Graphic organizers

Hint cards/hint folders

Icons or pictures that support understanding

Manipulatives

Minilessons/workshops

Modeling

Peer partners

Reading partners with appropriate materials and guidelines for working together

Recorded task directions or texts

Small-group instruction

Study guides

Teaching in multiple modalities

Text digests

Text in student's first language

Think-alouds

Voice-to-text programs

Websites that provide texts at varied Lexile levels

of their work, and so on. Different students will be ready for differing amounts of responsibility at any given time, but all students need to be guided in assuming a growing degree of responsibility and independence as learners and as members of a community of learners. Not only is that essential in a differentiated classroom, but it's a significant part of success in life outside the classroom as well.

The teacher sets the tone. It is a heavy responsibility and a wonderful opportunity to help students shape positive lives. As all people do, teachers have good days and ones they'd rather not duplicate. While none of us will ever do everything in the way of building a positive classroom environment exactly like we'd have chosen to do it if we could have scripted events, we can get better and better at modeling what we want students to learn—joy in work, appreciation of one another, patience, kindness, and generous hearts. Those things help students contribute to classroom community and construct sturdier and more rewarding lives now and at any age. Working toward those attributes helps the teacher become a wiser person and better professional as well.

Paving the Way for Respect and Success

In addition to the general guidance offered above, there are two concrete practices that can help teachers create a positive learning environment in a differentiated classroom: (1) teaching students to work productively in groups, and (2) planning for flexible grouping. Both practices rely on students being able to collaborate successfully.

Continually coach students to be contributing members of a group. As teachers, we often work in isolation and get little firsthand experience with effectively functioning groups. Sometimes, the best way to figure out how to help students succeed in small-group settings is just to study groups at work in your classroom and try to list the traits of functional versus dysfunctional groups. Then create tasks and give directions that steer students toward the more functional ways of working. Remember that students can help you develop groups that are productive if you involve them in goal setting, reflection, and problem solving. Figure 5.2 (see page 48) provides a few guidelines for establishing productive groups. Figure 5.3 (see page 49) shows a range of grouping activities.

In general, remember that groups will work better if students know what to do, how to do it, what is expected of group members, and what will constitute quality in both working processes and in products. Also reflect on the fact that an effective task will call for a meaningful contribution from every group member. That is not likely to occur when some members of the group have all the answers and skills and others clearly have a comparative deficit in knowledge and skills. Groups should not establish

---

Figure 5.2 A Checklist for Planning Effective Group Work

☐ Students understand the task goals—what they should know, understand, and be able to do as a result of their work with the task.

☐ The task is well-aligned with the goals—guides students to what they should know, understand, and be able to do.

☐ Students understand what is expected of each group member to make the group function effectively.

☐ The task is designed to be interesting/meaningful to the students.

☐ The task draws on group members' strengths and interests to ensure an important contribution from each group member.

☐ The task is designed to be challenging to the group members.

☐ The task requires group collaboration to achieve shared understanding and quality outcomes.

☐ Students understand routines and expectations for getting and returning materials, use of materials and supplies, moving around the room, conversation levels, getting help, and so on.

☐ Timelines are specified and brisk (but not rigid or impossible).

☐ Each student is responsible for individual understanding of all facets of the task.

☐ There's a respectful "way out" for students who are not succeeding with the group.

☐ There is built-in opportunity for teacher and/or peer coaching and in-process quality checks.

☐ Students understand what to do next if they complete their work early and at a high level of quality.

---

a caste system whereby some students are always the teachers and others are always the taught. You and your students can prevent this by developing tasks that call on the strengths of each member of the group so that the task cannot be accomplished as effectively if any member is disengaged (Cohen & Lotan, 2014). Also remember to have a respectful "way out" of the group for a student who cannot, at that particular moment, succeed with the group, even with your assistance and the assistance of the group. This alternative should not be punitive; it should simply present a different work setting—one that is more likely to support the student's success at the time.

Plan with flexible grouping in mind. In a differentiated classroom, you will often design tasks for students based on your best current evidence of their readiness for and interest in those tasks, as well as how they might work most effectively with the tasks. At such times, you may want to

---

Figure 5.3 Some Instructional Arrangements Within a Differentiated Classroom

1. Whole-Class Activities

- Pre-assessment of readiness/interest
- Content/skill introduction
- Teaching/modeling skills
- Troubleshooting
- Planning
- Discussing
- Sharing
- Wrap-up/closure

2. Individual or Personalized Activities

- Reading/listening
- Sense making
- Practice/skill application
- Homework
- Skill/interest centers
- Product/performance tasks
- Independent inquiry
- Formative and summative assessment

3. Teacher-Student Conferences

- Formative assessment
- Goal setting and planning
- Guidance and mentoring
- Troubleshooting

4. Small-Group Activities (Pairs, Triads, Quads)

- Sense making
- Teaching/modeling skills
- Shared reading
- Planning/task execution
- Group inquiry

---

assign students to an appropriate task based on observation and formative assessment information. At other times, you may want students to quickly discuss an idea with a nearby or pre-assigned thinking partner. Or it may be more convenient to have students work with others at their table or to turn their desks into a cluster of four students. You may want students to select their own task partners or opt to work alone. Nearly always, it's helpful to briefly explain the reasoning behind your chosen tasks, groupings, and routines so that students understand work patterns to be purposeful and designed with their interests in mind.

Using a variety of grouping strategies allows a teacher to match students and tasks when necessary, and to observe and assess students in a variety of groupings and task conditions. This flexibility also keeps students from feeling that they are "pegged" into a given classroom niche. During the course of a unit, there will be times when it makes most sense for students of a similar readiness level to work together or with the teacher. There should be other times when tasks are designed to bring together students of differing readiness levels in a way that will be meaningful to each member in the group. There will be times when students with similar interests should work together on a shared area of interest and times when students with different specialties can come together to look at an idea or topic from several different angles.

While use of similar-readiness groups is relatively familiar in classrooms, teachers may have less familiarity with heterogeneous groups that are specifically designed to engage each member in the group in ways that benefit each member (in contrast to heterogeneous groups in which some students feel competent and some incompetent with the assignment). It's particularly important that assignments designed for groups that are heterogeneous in terms of student readiness be interesting and relevant to all students in the group and that the assignments be designed to call on specific strengths or abilities of every student in the group (Cohen & Lotan, 2014).

It's also important that students understand how to work together in respectful and productive ways. For example, in his high school math classes, Ginsburg (2015) asked students to engage together in "productive struggle" through a "hierarchy of help plan" in heterogeneous groups. Students first worked independently on assignments, using their best thinking to address complex problems. Next, students consulted with one another, sharing ideas and seeking guidance. Only if everyone in the group was stuck could they ask the teacher for help. Differentiated classrooms offer prime opportunities for students from a broad range of backgrounds to learn from and teach one another. That happens, however, only when teachers carefully construct and guide learning opportunities designed to ensure equity of access to high-quality learning experiences that work for all members of the group.

As Figure 5.3 suggests, teachers in a differentiated classroom plan for flexible grouping at the outset of a unit, asking themselves, for example, "When during the unit should the class work as a whole? When should I plan small group activities? When does it make most sense for students to work individually? When should I plan time to meet with individuals?" Flexible grouping is central to showing respect for all learners, honoring individual differences, collaboration, and teaching for success in a differentiated classroom.

Figure 5.4 displays a teacher plan for six segments in a week-long unit on persuasive writing. Note the whole-class and small-group elements, with the latter including groupings based on similar and mixed readiness as well as on student interest and options for expressing learning.

Figure 5.4 An Excerpt of a Differentiated Lesson Plan at the Elementary Level

Whole-Class Activities	Differentiated Activities
Pre-assessment	
Think-Pair-Share on students' responses Discuss "persuasion" and what makes ideas/ writing persuasive Introduce elements of persuasive writing Analyze a persuasive paragraph for the elements, using a different color to mark each element—first as a whole class, then individually as an exit slip	
	Tiered lesson (four readiness-based tiers) on writing a persuasive paragraph Two small instructional groups—one for students whose writing is strong, to provide additional challenge; one for students who need additional support
Discuss and share examples of using evidence to support a persuasive argument—excerpts read by the teacher, projected text analyzed by the class, brief passages read by students with a reading buddy	
	Student practice using details to support persuasion based on interest (choice of topics), with resources based on readiness
Map an argument using an organizer and the key elements of persuasive writing	

Continued

Figure 5.4 An Excerpt of a Differentiated Lesson Plan at the Elementary Level—*continued*

Whole-Class Activities	Differentiated Activities
	In mixed-readiness "consultant" groups, students use an organizer to map out a persuasive argument based on interest (choice of teacher-proposed topic with an option for student-proposed topic). Students select a presentation format for their draft argument based on learning preference (choice of a storyboards, a recording, a list, a graphic organizer)
	Peer review/discussion of work using a checklist

Figure 5.5 presents a teacher plan for seven segments in a three-week middle school social studies unit on the Middle Ages, indicating whole-class, small-group, and individual work; flexible grouping; and use of varied instructional strategies to address student readiness, interest, and working arrangements. Note that both Figures 5.4 and 5.5 show only a portion of a unit plan.

Figure 5.5 An Excerpt of a Differentiated Lesson Plan at the Middle School Level

Whole-Class Activities	Differentiated Activities
Teacher introduces the Middle Ages using music, art, dance, recorded text, and fiction and nonfiction text excerpts (read by the teacher and student volunteers) with the focus question "What's familiar here and what's strange?"	
	Jigsaw activity on (a) castles and (b) life in the various positions of the feudal system to continue exploring life in the Middle Ages—resources at varied levels of sophistication available for all groups, including pictures, maps, videos, recordings, articles, websites, and books; jigsaw topic determined by student interest

Whole-Class Activities	Differentiated Activities
Sharing of jigsaw findings, focused on similarities and differences in students' cultures and the culture of the Middle Ages Homework: Teacher-prepared video minilecture/demonstration on the time period; viewing guide provided	
Class discussion of homework video in pre-assigned, mixed-readiness discussion teams that meet periodically through the unit, and with the class as a whole	
	Tiered reading: Text excerpts of varying complexity, assigned by readiness Readiness-based team discussion of readings; discussion protocol provided to support the conversation
Teacher introduction of a performance task that will serve as an end-of-unit summative assessment; students will work on this task for the remainder of the unit, drawing on what they learn through in- and out-of-class assignments	
	Learning stations focused on the writing skills required for the performance task; small-group assignment to stations are based on skills and needs demonstrated in past writing Teacher conferencing with small groups throughout station time for targeted writing work

The next chapter offers several scenarios of how teachers of different grade levels and subjects have used these guidelines to transform their role in the classroom and their students' learning experience.

6

A Look Inside Some Differentiated Classrooms

There is no recipe for a differentiated classroom. Teachers construct differentiated classrooms in varying ways depending on their own personalities, the nature of the subjects and grade levels they teach, and the learning needs of their students. Teachers who differentiate instruction have at least two things in common, however: a conviction that students differ as learners, and a belief that classrooms in which students are active learners, decision makers, and problem solvers are more natural and effective than those in which students are passive recipients of information.

Although there is no formula for differentiation, taking a glimpse at some differentiated classrooms is often helpful in envisioning how the principles of differentiation can be applied. The following tour includes approaches to differentiation appropriate for all grade levels and subjects. Differentiation will have a different feel in a high school class than in a primary one, of course, but the principles of differentiation apply across contexts.

Ms. Eames and Her 1st Graders

It's early spring, and Ms. Eames's 1st graders are sporting a wide range of reading levels as well as burgeoning interests in many different topics. One way Ms. Eames addresses both differences in her learners is with a flexible reading program. Each week, she posts a reading schedule. Students find their own names on the schedule and go to the appointed part of the room at times designated on the chart. In the course of the week, students are likely to read in as many as five or six configurations. There are always times when the whole class meets to listen to a story and talk about it, or to volunteer to read parts of the story aloud. Sometimes a small group of students meets with Ms. Eames to work on decoding, comprehension strategies, or talking about reading just for the pleasure of sharing ideas. At other points, students meet with peers who want to read on a topic of mutual interest, regardless of their reading readiness. There may be books at different reading levels on the same topic, or students may read varying portions of the same material. Students also read alone—sometimes from discovery boxes, which they can browse for books of interest on a number of topics, and sometimes from boxes of books designated with a color and matching their reading level. There are always many books at different reading levels that represent a variety of cultures and backgrounds representative of students in the class. Sometimes students meet with a read-aloud partner. In these instances, they may take turns reading, or Ms. Eames may ask them to "choral read" or "echo read" so that a stronger reader can provide leadership for a peer who does not yet read quite as well.

This sort of flexible reading arrangement enables the teacher to target particular teaching needs, provide for interest-based explorations, have students share both their skills and interests with a good range of classmates, and work with the class as a whole on reading.

Mrs. Riley and Her 3rd Graders

Mrs. Riley uses a number of differentiation strategies, but one she finds quite natural is the use of learning centers and interest centers. Based on an assumption that all learners need exposure to the same content, she used to create centers and then send each child to every center. Now, after designing a variety of centers based on her students' current points of development with key knowledge, understandings, and skills, Mrs. Riley often assigns students to specific centers based on her formal and informal assessment of their readiness. There are also points in the center activities when students make choices about their work in ways that address their interests and preferred ways of expressing what they are learning.

Today, for example, all students will be assigned to one of two reading/writing learning centers. Both centers focus on biographies the students have read. At each center, students can elect to work alone, with a partner, or with a group of three or four peers assigned to their center.

At one center, students select a person they've read about and make an annotated timeline of the person's childhood, selecting events that they think were most important in shaping the person's life. Then they choose to write about their chosen person and these formative events, draw a storyboard illustrating the events and their impact, or act out the events one day during sharing time. Whatever way a student decides to express understanding, the focus must be on identifying themes or patterns in the life of the person about whom they read.

At the other, more complex reading/writing center, students select one of the biographies they've read as well as a fictional work they've read about a young person. Then they write about some real-life events that they and some of their 3rd grade friends have experienced. Finally, after looking in all three works for common themes about growing up, they design a method of showing how those themes are present in each. Mrs. Riley gives them three product suggestions: theme trees; a matrix; and conversations among the subject of the biography, the fictional character, and a 3rd grader. There are examples of each mode of expression at the centers.

Some students go early in the day to one of these two reading/writing centers; after that, they work individually with differentiated math assignments at their desks or in small groups. Other students experience this combination of activities in reverse order.

Mrs. Riley also sets up a rotating series of interest centers, which allow students to explore topics like acting, how to make storyboards, and how to use an app to create an animation, in addition to science- and math-related topics. She's careful to stock these with content reflecting the contributions from varied cultures, races, and economic backgrounds. Interest centers are available at various times during the week. Students select which interest centers to attend, and Mrs. Riley keeps an eye on who gravitates to which topics; this is good information that she can use. Most interest centers in Mrs. Riley's classroom are available for two to four weeks. Students often make suggestions for interest centers and sometimes contribute materials for the centers.

Mr. Blackstone and His 6th Graders

Mr. Blackstone teaches science to students in his middle school. This week, the students are beginning a study of inertia. To introduce the unit, Mr. Blackstone gathers the whole class together and uses a variety of media and demonstrations to ensure that all students have a grasp of key vocabulary and ideas related to inertia. Next, the students do some shared reading with texts and websites at varied reading levels (and, as appropriate/feasible, in students' first languages), continuing the exploration of inertia and how it works in the world. Later, students learn more about inertia by working at one of two labs designed to help them understand, analyze, and apply important unit-related principles. One lab employs a more multifaceted, complex, and ambiguous problem than the other, but both labs call on students to apply what they are learning to address a real-world problem. The teacher assigns students to the lab he feels is most appropriate for them, based on observation of the students over time, dialogue during the whole-class introduction, and "exit cards" summarizing the key principles of inertia that all students submitted after the whole-class introduction and the shared readings.

Guided by information gathered through these exit cards and ongoing formative assessment, Mr. Blackstone continues a whole-class exploration of the topic, with a focus on clearing up misunderstandings or gaps in understanding that have come to light. Students then complete a differentiated homework assignment designed to focus on either consolidating or extending their understanding of inertia.

At the end of the week, students take a formal assessment that gauges how well they've learned the key principles from their whole-class studies, readings, differentiated labs, and homework. This assessment is also formative. Students who show mastery on the test begin working on a rocketry project, either alone or with one or two other classmates who have also shown mastery. Students who do not yet show mastery begin working on a more structured rocketry project, designed to ensure that they revisit and apply the key principles. Mr. Blackstone works closely with this group of students, probing and guiding their thinking so they can apply important understandings. He also works periodically with the more advanced group on their project, pushing their thinking further. Through his work with small groups, which takes up a large portion of overall class time, Mr. Blackstone gets to know his students and how they think. Because he enjoys both his subject and his students, the students enjoy working with him and look forward to both whole-class and small-group work. In both settings, they feel they have his attention and support.

Ms. Jeffries and Her 8th Grade History Students

Ms. Jeffries is determined to help her students understand that history is a living thing, so her 8th graders often work on investigative projects that help them explore themes common to history that transcend time and place.

She has designed a project to help them explore what went on in their Virginia town during the U.S. Civil War. All students begin this project by reading material available in class, viewing videos, and doing some guided library and Internet research. During these activities, they log information they will use as background material for their projects. Next, they make individual selections of resources from a menu of print, video, and web references their teacher and the media specialist have prepared. In individual conversations, Ms. Jeffries often adds one or two additional resources to a student's list based on her assessment of that learner's reading/comprehension levels, as well as on her sense of topics they might enjoy. Students also have to find at least one source of information that is not in their classroom or school library. (Ms. Jeffries's source list includes possibilities such as talking with teachers in the school, interviewing students who have completed the study in previous years, or going to a nearby public library or museum.)

As students conduct their in-class or library research, Ms. Jeffries encourages them to share with one another in a round-robin discussion both sources and ideas they find interesting. Students also keep a running class list of topics that they might explore for their investigations, such as medical practice in their town during the Civil War, disease patterns, the local Civil War economy, the architecture and buildings in the town then and now, roles of local citizens in the military, local politics during that period, and schooling or education during the Civil War. Within two to four days, students decide on a first and second choice for their investigation, which they submit to their teacher.

Ms. Jeffries then assigns students to groups, based on topics and strengths. Sometimes she constructs mixed-readiness groups of five or six students; other times, she pairs students who have common interests and work well together. Flexible grouping allows her to tailor projects for students based on their levels of independence, background knowledge, comprehension levels, and interests.

A key principle in Ms. Jeffries's class, however, is the importance of working as colleagues. Students in one group are free to call on students in any other group for advice or assistance with a specific task, such as computer work, drawing, animating, or editing. She also pairs students across groups every few days so they can share ideas that might benefit other students doing similar investigations. The tone is one of cooperation for mutual success, not competition for scarce rewards. Ms. Jeffries negotiates with her students to determine the criteria for the content, format, and quality of final products. Some criteria apply to the class as a whole, while others are specific to a group or individual task.

Ms. Jeffries designed this Civil War project carefully. It has both clearly defined, "custom-fit" responsibilities for each student, and vague, unassigned components that each group must work out how to handle. Every student has an opportunity to make a clear, individual contribution to the whole that is personally challenging and interesting. And all students engage in tasks that help them improve their negotiating and group-work skills. She takes care to integrate required knowledge and skills throughout all elements of student work, but also believes that students will learn more deeply and more enthusiastically through inquiry and product-focused learning than through rote memorization of great amounts of data that can be disconnected from one another and from students' lives.

Mr. Morales and His High School Math Students

Mr. Morales has found that by the time students enter Algebra II, their levels of math skill are quite varied. Some students seem to grasp the principles in a chapter almost before they encounter them in class; others look squint-eyed and genuinely puzzled as their peers put homework answers on the board or propose solutions in whole-class discussions. Somewhere in the middle are students who grasp the ideas but typically require multiple learning experiences to do so.

When Mr. Morales used whole-class instruction and common homework as the primary way to address everyone's needs, he found that many of his students were frustrated and discouraged, while others were bored with the pace. So he began thinking of his class differently. Now, when beginning a new topic, he pre-assesses his students to get an early sense of their comfort with key prerequisite knowledge and skills and the approaches they use to tackle new ideas from the upcoming content. He front-loads vocabulary for students whose academic vocabulary in the topic appears weak and continues to actively support vocabulary for them throughout the unit.

He also uses more student-focused whole-class exploration of ideas behind the operations, raising questions and encouraging students to propose ideas, question one another, offer alternative suggestions, and be ready to challenge assertions he makes during discussions. His goal is to cast all of the students as thinkers and problem solvers—independently and in collaboration with one another. Throughout whole-class sessions, which are now shorter in duration than they once were, Mr. Morales uses a variety of pairs, triads, and quads to have students share ideas, approaches, and questions with one another.

Following whole-class investigations, he sometimes offers students two or three options for practice, indicating that if they feel they'd benefit most from additional practice with "Skill A," they might want to work alone or with one or two classmates on "Assignment A"; if they feel they'd benefit most from additional practice with "Skill B," they might select "Assignment B," and so on. As students work, he moves continually among the groups, asking questions and clarifying ideas.

At other times, he provides mixed-readiness groups of four with "Brain Buster" problems that ask for solutions or "plans of attack" in a relatively limited time. Mr. Morales sets up these challenging problems so that the solution won't be readily evident to any of the students; they must all pull together to find solutions or offer methods of addressing the problem. Mr. Morales makes a big deal of groups that collaborated effectively, engaging everyone in their deliberations, and he points out both productive and nonproductive group strategies he observes as the groups work to move their thinking forward.

Sometimes he provides two, three, or four tiered tasks for groups of three or four students arranged by readiness based on a previous day's formative assessment matching the task to their current performance levels. On still other occasions, he develops interest-based problems for student consideration. At these times, Mr. Morales will indicate that students can select a problem related to basketball, for example, or making money, interior design, assigning grades, and so on. The topics change often and continue to reflect a variety of subjects he knows interest his students as he comes to understand them in greater detail.

Sometimes he assigns differentiated homework. Sometimes he asks students to select one of two or three homework assignments they feel will most likely help with their continuing growth in the ideas and skills they are working with in class. Sometimes students all do the same homework assignment.

Mr. Morales has found that his new approach to his classes is much more effective in terms of both student engagement and student mastery of important insights and competencies. He also knows his students and understands their learning trajectories much better than in the past. He says he feels like he and his students are now partners in success, and that roles feels much more fulfilling to him.

The Teacher's Toolbox

These five teachers use a variety of instructional strategies to help them match content, process, and product to the readiness, interest, and talents of their academically diverse students. Among the strategies described were pre-assessment and formative assessment, interest centers and learning centers, small-group instruction, interest-based resources, alternating similar-readiness and mixed-readiness working groups, tiered lessons, student choice, student discussion and problem-solving groups, options for varied modes of expression, front-loading vocabulary, differentiated homework, reading materials at varied levels of complexity, peer reading partners (reading buddies), and peer reviews. See the Appendix for a descriptive list of some of these and other instructional strategies that are useful for addressing varied learners' needs in a differentiated classroom.

The next chapter offers 18 "megastrategies" you can use to move away from one-size-fits-all instruction and toward designing instruction that meets students where they are and helps them move ahead through appropriate challenge, attention to their interests, and approaches to learning.

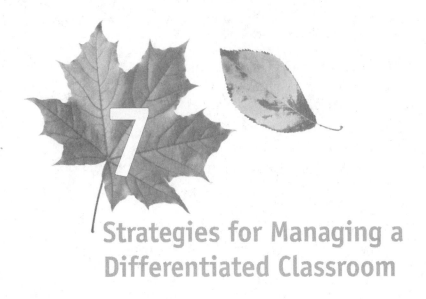

Strategies for Managing a Differentiated Classroom

For some teachers, uncertainty about how to manage a differentiated classroom grows into a fear that stops them from even attempting to provide instruction based on their students' varied interests and needs. Many teachers don't appreciate just how skilled they are at classroom management—at attending to multiple signals and juggling a variety of roles. The truth is, teachers can leverage the same skills that they're accustomed to using in their classroom today to move toward success in a differentiated classroom environment.

Benefits for Students and Teachers

As Piaget (1978) reflected, "The heartbreaking difficulty in pedagogy, as indeed in medicine and other branches of knowledge that partake at the same time of art and science, is, in fact, that the best methods are also the most difficult ones" (p. 69). Although managing a differentiated classroom is not always easy, progress in that direction tends to make school a better fit for more students. It also tends to make teaching more satisfying and invigorating.

Managing a Differentiated Classroom: The Basics

Worthwhile endeavors are often challenging—and usually worth it. Here are 18 key strategies you can use to successfully meet the challenge of designing and managing differentiated instruction for your learners. (See also Tomlinson & Imbeau, 2010.)

1. Have a strong rationale for creating a differentiated classroom—and share it with students and their parents. Just as teachers sometimes need help creating new mental images of classrooms as places that are fluid and offer many avenues to learning, so do students and parents. If you help both your students and their parents understand and contribute to your new view of the classroom, they will be your best colleagues. Without this kind of leadership, they may feel that you are "violating the rules of the game," which could leave them confused or resistant. Leadership that elicits understanding, contribution, and support from students and parents is so important that the next chapter will more fully describe a way to prepare yourself, your students, and their caretakers for a student-focused classroom.

2. Study your students. No teacher will ever have full knowledge of his or her students, but a teacher who studies students from day one, with the intent to continue developing insights about each child throughout the year, will be in a far better position to teach them well than a teacher who does not have that priority or a teacher who concludes that there are too many students to know them as individuals. There's no explicit formula for learning about students, but there are a number of good approaches to try.

Greet students as they come in the door, and say good-bye to them as they leave the room each day. Make a bit of time to talk informally with the class as often as you can, and work to hear from each student in those conversations at least over the course of a week. At the same time, cultivate good listening skills, and try to "listen beyond the words" as students talk to you and to one another. Continually observe students as they work, making notes that can help you with instructional planning.

Take special care to learn about the cultures, languages, and background experiences of students whose lives may differ markedly from your own. Ask students about their interests, what's working in the class for them, and things they'd like you to consider changing or improving. Seek students' input on assignments and classroom routines. Whenever possible, be present during extracurricular activities and take note of who your students are when they are outside your classroom. And make families your partners as often as you can. After just a few years of experience, a teacher of 2nd graders or high school juniors is likely to have more insight into kids of those ages than a parent does, but a good parent will always have greater depth of knowledge about his or her child than a teacher can have. The union of depth and breadth can be hugely instructive when parents and a teacher work together to benefit a young person.

3. Begin differentiating at a pace that is comfortable for you. Some teachers already make frequent adjustments in curriculum and instruction to allow for student differences in their classrooms. With just a few additional insights, these teachers are ready to move ahead to a full differentiation. Others who are less experienced or confident need to make this move in smaller increments. There's a strong parallel to students in a classroom here. Some will leap like leopards through a given task; others will move at a more measured gait. What matters most is that students—and teachers—make progress from their respective beginning points, not that they all work alike. As a teacher notes in *Absolutely Almost* (Graff, 2014), you can't get where you're going without being where you are. This is as true for teachers as it is for the young learners in our charge.

You may easily envision yourself working with varied learning resources, such as diverse texts, multilevel supplementary materials, various computer programs, apps, or peer tutors. On the other hand, you may feel more comfortable using a single text with your class but allowing some students to move through it more rapidly or differentiating activities so students gain an understanding of its ideas at their own pace. Perhaps you'd find it easiest to differentiate student products or performance tasks. Or perhaps creating small-group tasks tailored to student readiness, interest, or particular student talents might be more your style. Maybe you could begin by learning to use groups in your class—not varying the group tasks at first, but just gaining skill and confidence in directing groups.

If you teach multiple subjects, you may want to try your hand first in the subject you enjoy most. If you teach different groups of students each day, you might find it advantageous to begin differentiating instruction for the group you find easiest to work with. All this is to say that finding your point of readiness and beginning there is key. Not beginning at all is a guaranteed way to avoid progress. Biting off too much invites discouragement and failure. Begin where you can, and chart a timeline for your own progress.

Figure 7.1 lists some approaches to differentiation that tend to take less preparation time from teachers and others that are likely to require more preparation time.

Figure 7.1 Some Low-Prep and Higher-Prep Instructional Strategies for Differentiation

Low-Prep Differentiation Strategies

- Choices of books/reading materials
- Classroom discussions with questions at varied complexity levels
- Design-a-Day work options
- Flexible seating
- Front-loading vocabulary
- Games/apps for mastery of information, skills, and language
- Homework options with homework checkers
- Joint teacher and student goalsetting
- Let's Make a Deal options for products or formats of daily tasks
- Materials in students' first languages
- Materials inclusive of varied cultures
- Materials to add depth and breadth to learning
- Minilessons/workshops to reteach, clarify, extend
- Open-ended activities
- Options for varied note-taking and organizing formats
- Personalized computer programs for practice
- Range of materials at varied readability levels
- Range of materials based on varied interests
- Range of media for taking in information
- Reading buddies
- Seeking multiple perspectives on issues
- Show & Tell options
- Story frames, sentence frames, paragraph frames
- Student goal setting
- Translation apps
- Use of small-group sharing (e.g., Think-Pair-Share)
- Using podcasts with scripts to support reading comprehension
- Varied options for expressing learning
- Varying collaboration, independence, competition
- Varying pacing with anchor options
- Varying writing prompts
- Websites providing texts at varied Lexile levels
- Whole-to-part and part-to-whole explanations
- Word maps
- Work alone or with a partner options

Higher-Prep Differentiation Strategies

- Assignment checklists/guides
- Choice boards (assignment boards)
- Community mentorships
- Compacting
- Complex Instruction/groupworthy tasks
- Contemporary lecture
- Content digests
- Differentiated interest centers
- Differentiated learning centers
- Differentiating with technology
- Entry points
- Jigsaws
- Learning contracts (including menus, Think-Tac-Toe, BINGOs, learning agendas)
- Learning Stations
- Literature Circles/Learning Circles
- Longer-term explorations/independent investigations based on student interest
- Personal agendas
- Picturing writing
- Problem-based learning
- Project-based learning
- RAFTS assignments
- Sidebar studies
- Specialty groups/expert groups
- Think Dots
- Tiered activities, labs, or products/performance assessments
- Tri-Mind options (Sternberg intelligences)
- Varied graphic organizers

A good way to become comfortable with differentiation without it taking over your life is to select a few low-prep strategies to use consistently during a year, and then choose one high-prep approach per unit or quarter to add to your repertoire. During a second year of differentiation implementation, you can hone the low- and high-prep approaches from the previous year and add one or two more high- and low-prep approaches. In that cumulative way, you can work your way to a highly differentiated classroom in four or five years without feeling absolutely frenzied.

4. Time differentiated activities to support student success. Some students can manage group or independent work for long periods of time. Others have less capacity to sustain group or independent tasks. When designing your tasks, remember two things: (1) time allotted for a task should be a bit less than the attention span of the students who work on that task, so that they both remain engaged and feel some sense of urgency for completing the work, and (2) advanced learners often have extended attention spans.

When designing tasks for students with strong interest and ability in a particular area, it can be helpful to allow a larger chunk of time during a class, day, or week than you would if designing the task for students whose interest or talent in the same area is currently not as great. It would seem natural to assume advanced learners would need less time and struggling learners need more. Often that's the case. But there are occasions when it's wisest to ensure that a struggling learner works with just the core of complex content before moving ahead, and occasions when an advanced learner benefits greatly from additional time that allows for deeper or broader exploration. The goal you're working toward is to help all students sustain group and independent tasks for increased periods of time, and the key to reaching that goal is increasing every student's sense of success in those tasks.

5. Use "anchor activities" to address "ragged time" and free you to provide focused attention on students. Because having all students finish all tasks at the same time is not a goal of differentiation, "ragged time"—periods where some students have finished while others are still working—is a reality in a differentiated classroom. Having certain independent "anchor activities" to which students automatically move when they complete an assigned task is important both to maintaining a productive work environment and to ensuring wise use of everyone's time. Reading, journal writing, creating a portfolio of work samples (paper or digital), and practicing (spelling, computation, vocabulary, writing, art techniques, language sounds or speech patterns, skills in a sport, etc.) are the sorts of tasks that are well-suited to this purpose.

Begin by teaching your whole class to work independently and quietly on one or two of these practice-focused activities. Then move to having half of the class work on the anchor activity (which can be adjusted to student readiness and interest), while the other half engages in a different content-based activity designed specifically for their needs. This strategy can help you feel less fragmented in the beginning stages of differentiation, because a sizable portion of the class will be engaged in work that is largely self-directed, freeing you to guide students in the newer and "less predictable" task. Later on, you can flip-flop the class, having the group that first worked with the anchor activity switch to an appropriate content-based activity and vice versa. Then, when you feel ready, you can have a third of the class working with an anchor activity and two-thirds working with two differentiated content-based tasks. All sorts of combinations are possible. Do whatever feels best to phase you and your students into an environment where multiple avenues to learning are the norm and where the work proceeds smoothly.

Ultimately, your aim is to have all students understand that when they complete a given assignment, they must automatically move to an anchor activity and work on that activity with care and concentration. Be sure to encourage students to suggest and contribute to anchor activities, too, as you expand anchor activities from a practice orientation to richer, more meaning-driven tasks that support deeper understanding of and engagement with key principles or big ideas of the content students are studying.

6. Create and deliver instructions carefully. Giving multiple sets of directions to the class as a whole can be confusing and can call too much attention to who is doing what. A better alternative is creating and giving task cards or assignment sheets to individuals or groups. Another option is going over an assignment with a few responsible students today so that they can share directions with their groups tomorrow. Similarly, each group may have a designated "directions reader" whose job includes answering peers' questions about directions. It can also be helpful to record directions, especially when they are complex, so students can replay them as needed. Students who are learning English might benefit from directions that are written more simply, with bulleted steps and more white space on the page—or from directions written in their first language, when that is feasible. Recorded and simplified directions are also handy for students with reading or sequencing problems.

Be sure you've thought through directions carefully, have anticipated student questions or sticking points, and have struck a balance between clarity and challenge. When part of the directions require students to move to another place in the classroom, let students know how much time they have to get there, and provide clear expectations for what constitutes orderly movement. Less transit time is generally preferable to more transit time, but you don't want students dashing around the classroom or running into one another. Always share your rational for directions and routines with students.

7. Create a system for assigning students to groups or seating areas. It's awkward and confusing to call students' names in order to send them to various seating areas or to assign them to particular groups. You'll find it is smoother to list names by color or group on a board or screen that also indicates where the colors or groups should report. Wall charts work well also, especially for groups that will have a somewhat extended duration. For young students, pegboards and key tags with students' names on them allow you to "move" students to a learning center or section of the room flexibly and with ease.

8. Have a "home base" for students. Beginning and ending a class or lesson from a "home base" or established seating plan enables you to organize students and materials more effectively when there will be student movement during the class or lesson. In middle and high school classes, assigned home-base seats also allow you to check attendance without "calling the roll" and provide a mechanism for ensuring that materials and supplies are put away appropriately for the next class before you dismiss students in the current class.

9. Have a plan for students to get help when you're busy with another student or group. Be sure students know when it's OK to come to you for help—and when it's not—and that there are several options for finding help when you are unavailable. For differentiated instruction to succeed, students must understand that it's never OK for them to just sit and wait for help to come to them or to disrupt someone else through off-task behavior, and that it's each student's responsibility to seek and to offer help in responsible ways as needed.

You can help students learn to work collegially by suggesting that they ask a peer for clarification when they get stuck. Some classrooms have an "expert of the day" desk where one or more students especially skilled with the day's task serve as consultants. Astute teachers ensure that all students serve as "experts" at one time or another. (Students can assist by checking answers, proofreading, answering questions about directions or texts, and helping with art or construction tasks.) Or students may try to get themselves unstuck by "thinking on paper" in learning logs, for example.

10. Minimize noise. When students do meaningful work in a classroom, there will be some noise, but there is no need for the noise to become oppressive. From the beginning of the year, provide students with guidance on how to work with peers at a level of conversation that's productive without being distracting. Teach them to whisper or talk softly. Use a signal (such as turning the light on and off quickly, a hand signal, or a small chime) to remind them to reduce the conversation level. Assign a student in each group to monitor the noise level and remind peers to talk softly.

Some students in your class may be especially sensitive to noise. Finding a section of the room somewhat removed from the noise may be helpful for them. If that is not adequate, permitting the use of headphones or earplugs (such as those used on airplanes to dampen sound) can make a difference as well. Remember to involve students in conversation about balancing their needs for conversation and concentration, and let them help you find other ways to address both.

11. Make a plan for how students will turn in work. There are times in a differentiated classroom when multiple tasks are going on at once, and when various students may turn in several different assignments in a relatively short time span. It is distracting for you and the students with whom you're working when other students come to you to hand over their finished pieces. Try using "experts of the day" or "student checkers" who can check over a piece of work a student believes is finished to see if it is both complete and of good quality. If the "expert" concurs that the work is ready to be turned in, have the "expert" sign the paper and have the student place it in a box or file labeled with the name of the task or an appropriate icon in a predesignated place in the room. If the "expert" feels the work is incomplete or lacking in quality, the student must continue working on the piece until the existing issues are appropriately addressed.

12. Teach students to rearrange the furniture. You can draw three or four floor plans with furniture arranged differently in each one, post those plans on a bulletin board or on the wall, and teach the students how to move the furniture quickly and quietly to correspond with the floor plan you designate (by name, number, or color). That makes you feel freer to be flexible with room arrangements than if you personally must move all the furniture each time it's rearranged. Be clear about your expectations for orderly movement, and also help students understand how the variety of configurations will contribute to more interesting, successful, and rewarding classwork.

13. Minimize "stray" movement. Kids need to move around, regardless of their age, and in a differentiation classroom, it's rarely a goal to keep everyone glued to his or her chair. On the other hand, an undue amount of idle roaming isn't likely to come to a good end. Think through the amount of movement you will be comfortable with, and let your students know what they can and can't do. For example, it may be fine for students to get up and go to an "expert of the day" if they're stuck on a math problem—but only as long as the expert isn't already working with someone else. Or it may be that you want to designate a "gopher" for each work group who will get materials needed for the day's work, noting that only the gopher should be up from the table and perhaps that only one group's gopher can be up at any one time. It's also often wise to physically separate the materials and supplies accessible to students from those that should be accessed only by the teacher. In general, the purpose of structuring student movement is to keep you and the students feeling productive.

14. Promote on-task behavior. Help your students understand that you value on-task behavior because it helps them do better-quality work, helps you concentrate on what you need to do to help them, and reduces distractions for others. Be sure to clarify what you mean by on-task behavior for a particular assignment—some work may call for silence, some for using quiet conversation, some for movement within a portion of the classroom, and so on. If your standards for "being on task" are different from those of the students, they may feel they are working just fine when you think otherwise.

It's to be expected that some students will need extra support in this area. You may want to let students know that you will be giving them a daily check on how well they are using their time. You can make a list of students who are working with extra concentration and put a plus by their names. Similarly, you can make a list of students who find it very difficult to stay on task, even after coaching from you and reminders from peers, and put a minus beside those names. Most students most days will do fine. Later, you can fill the pluses and minuses into a spreadsheet or ledger, then add checks by everyone else's name. Most days, there will be mostly checks. Letting your students look at their pattern over a period of a week or month can help them see how you're assessing their concentration. The patterns in the students' concentration also provide good assessment information for you. They may indicate a student who is frustrated because work is too hard or too easy, a student who needs a different seating arrangement, or a student who is really taking off with his or her work. In general, this sort of record of student focus should be used as a conversation point with students (and perhaps parents) but should not be incorporated into grades—unless your report card contains a specific place to record a process/habits-of-mind-and-work grade. In the latter instance, a record of on-task behaviors is one example of data that can capture how a student contributes (or doesn't contribute) to his or her own success.

15. Have a plan for "quick finishers." Students who consistently complete their work early, and do so with competence, are providing you with a clear indication that tasks are insufficiently challenging. (There will also be bright students who lollygag in the hope that you don't notice how easy the work is for them; this can feel safer than signaling a need for something more complex that they might not find as easy.) But not all quick finishers fit this profile. Sometimes the task is at the right challenge level, but students rush through it in order to be "the first one done." With these quick finishers, it's important to convey that you understand that they are competent with the task, but that what you're interested in seeing from them is "knock your socks off" quality. Ask them to tell you several indicators or characteristics of superior thought and craftsmanship on the piece of work and then to improve the quality of their work by applying some of those indicators before turning it in again. Feel free to contribute some indicators yourself. Try not to accept work that doesn't show a student aspiring to quality and taking pride in their work. (Remember, however, that students are unlikely to take pride in work that lacks purpose, relevance, and meaning.)

16. Make a plan for "calling a halt." While you will want to use time flexibly in a differentiated classroom, there will be a point in every lesson sequence or unit when you need to bring closure. There may still be students not yet finished, and it's important to think through how you will handle that. Some helpful approaches include giving students advance warning (a day or two ahead of time, for example) of when the deadline will be, providing alternative homework assignments so students who want to can have a night or two to finish the work at home, using a learning contract or anchor activity time to allow for some additional work, or asking individual students to help you figure out how they can complete unfinished work, even as the class moves on.

17. Give your students as much responsibility for their learning as possible. Not only does fostering student responsibility make classroom management far more effective, it also helps young learners become independent—an important learning goal on its own. Students can pass out folders and other materials, review one another's work, move furniture for group work, keep records of their own work, chart their progress by using established goals, choose topics or issues for independent or small-group investigation, help design some of their own tasks, make suggestions for smoother classroom operation, and so on. We often underestimate the capacity of students to be self-sufficient.

18. Engage your students in talking about classroom procedures and group processes. Your "metacognition," or thinking aloud about your thinking, helps students understand your expectations as well as the rationales for those expectations. It also helps them develop ownership in their classroom. Having ongoing conversations about what you're all experiencing individually and collectively is a great investment in the future, saving much more time and stress in the long run than these conversations require at the time. Besides, you'll be amazed at how many times the students can spot and think of a solution to a problem before you can figure it out. Use their eyes and minds to make the class work smoothly and comfortably for everyone.

There are many other effective ways to develop a classroom in which students engage in a variety of interesting and engaging activities. Share your management-of-differentiation strategies with colleagues and ask them to share with you what works for them.

Preparing Students and Parents for a Differentiated Classroom

In a differentiated classroom, some of the traditional ground rules about "how we do school" change. Your students and their parents—a category that includes all primary caregivers, such as grandparents, other custodial relatives, and legal guardians— may initially need your help to understand and feel comfortable with the new look and feel of the classroom. After an initial period of uncertainty, most students and parents respond quite positively to a setting that treats individuals as unique people and where learning is active and engaging. This chapter offers some strategies for making students and parents feel "at home" in a differentiated classroom.

Introducing Students to Differentiated Instruction: A Middle School Scenario

Mrs. Middleton begins every school year with a clear idea of how she wants her differentiated middle school English classes to work. Knowing she needs her students' input and help to reach that goal, she has developed an effective way to both orient her students to the environment she wants to create for them and enlist their help in creating it.

First, Mrs. Middleton shows her students how to make a line graph. They choose ways to describe the quality of something, which they then position as labels along the vertical axis. Each class chooses different descriptors, but the top (best) labels are often something like "awesome" or "spectacular." The bottom (worst) labels on the vertical axis tend to be something like "disastrous" or "dismal." Students also label several points in between the "best" and "worst" indicators.

Next, Mrs. Middleton asks the students to put descriptors along the horizontal axis, such as "good in writing," "good in math," "good in soccer," "good in reading," "good in cleaning my room," "good with poetry," "good in spelling." Some of these stem from topics or skills central to the subject she teaches. Others intentionally do not relate directly to English class. Then she asks the students to add two or three descriptors of their own choosing. To help her students understand how to plot themselves on their graph, she makes a graph of herself on the board while they watch. She plots herself as very strong with writing, somewhat strong with math, weaker with spelling, about average with soccer and cleaning her room, and so on. When she plots herself on each of her additional descriptors—"good with photography," "good with cartooning," and "good with crossword puzzles"—she discusses her interest in each area. Students complete their graphs for homework, and each day for the next couple of weeks, three or four students share their graphs with the class—spotlighting three or four items of particular interest. After they share their graphs, the students tape them on a classroom wall under a sign signifying their class period.

When all students have finished sharing their graphs, Mrs. Middleton asks them what patterns they see in the graphs, and she lists the ones they note. Students usually see several patterns quickly, especially the first two in the following list:

- Everybody said they are better in some things and worse in others.
- Nobody drew a flat line and said they were the same in everything.
- More girls than boys said they were good spellers.
- People mostly added things they were good at.

Mrs. Middleton takes a minute to reflect on their responses, and then she poses this question to her students: "If you are different in your strengths—strong in spelling and weak in reading, for example—what should I do about that?" Her students' response to this question is usually that she should work with them in different ways based on their needs. They often suggest that her main goal should be to help them all grow, and not just in their weaker areas but in their strong areas too. Sometimes they say that this means they should not all do the same tasks all the time in class. The 8th grade classes even offer her specific examples, such as giving advanced vocabulary assignments to students who already know a lot of the required vocabulary words, or giving shorter writing assignments to students who find writing very difficult, or letting students read the kinds of books they like as well as required ones.

Then, over several days, Mrs. Middleton engages her students in discussions about how the class will need to function if they are going to do different things in a single class period, and the students work with her to establish rules for a class like that. At some point, they discuss what "fair" will mean in their class and typically conclude that it will mean everyone gets the support they need to grow and succeed. Later in the marking period, they even discuss the most helpful ways of grading. They often decide that grades should reflect their individual progress, not just how they did on certain standards or what their average grade for the marking period was. Over time, students talk about setting individual goals in addition to goals for the whole class, how to keep track of their own work and progress, and how to help one another succeed.

Mrs. Middleton concludes this "preparation" phase by summarizing what they've all agreed is necessary for a class designed to help everyone grow as much as possible. She posts this summary in the front of the room. "I think we're agreeing," she says, "that we'll all live by the class rules, all of us will give our best effort to do quality work, and all of us will respect one another and encourage one another. Sometimes we'll all be doing the same thing, and sometimes we won't."

She lets her students know it is OK to come to her and say they'd really like to be working with a particular topic or project someone else is doing, or that what they're working on doesn't seem to be working for them. "Lots of times," she assures them, "I'll be able to let you know when a particular kind of assignment might be coming up for you. And we can often adjust work that doesn't seem to be a good fit so that it will be more helpful. My goal is to work with you to figure out what will make learning interesting and effective for you."

Within the first few days of the school year, Mrs. Middleton's students begin practicing the procedures for things like distributing work folders, student-choice reading, reading partners, individual conferences with the teacher, small-group tasks, peer review groups, and so on. Often, Mrs. Middleton takes some time to be "metacognitive" with her students. She asks them to assess (briefly) how the work they did as individuals and in small groups helped them achieve their work goals for the day or week, how the various routines worked for them, and which adjustments they'd suggest to make the routines more effective.

Mrs. Middleton makes certain to use all sorts of grouping arrangements and to help students understand her reasons for using particular groupings on specific days. She made an important discovery about her classroom management one day when she overheard a student say to a friend, "I think Mrs. Middleton stays up nights trying to figure out another way to scramble us up." After this comment, she began giving students more insight into her grouping strategies and more voice in making decisions about how and when various kinds of groups might be most advantageous to their progress. She says often, "Let me know if you think what you're doing is too hard or too easy for you, and I'll take a look at it with you. We can make changes when we need to so that as often as possible, your work is a good fit for you."

In school, just like everywhere else, there's likely no such thing as a perfect day, but Mrs. Middleton and her students have lots of very good days and few rough ones. Their classroom is a comfortable, busy, and respectful place—one that both the teacher and students work to create.

Introducing Students and Parents to Differentiation: A Primary Grade Scenario

Mr. Wade sends a survey home to parents early in the year, asking them to provide the approximate ages of their children when they began to do things like walking, talking, singing, riding a tricycle, dressing themselves, and so on. He charts the results and, not surprisingly, always finds that in every endeavor, some students accomplished various tasks well before or well after others. When he discusses these findings with the students in his class, he often asks, "Does it seem to matter much that somebody began talking nearly a year before someone else? Seems like everyone in here is talking fine now!" The students agree that *when* they began to talk is not nearly as important as that they *did* begin to talk. Mr. Wade uses that as a reminder in class that some students will learn to count higher and faster or read more comfortably sooner. That's fine, the students agree, as long as everyone is working on the skills they need to get better and better at doing important things.

When Mr. Wade speaks to parents at parents night, he muses about what would have happened had any of them tried to get their children to walk before they could stand, or run before they could walk. Or what if they had spent every day in a hovering panic because the child next door was talking and their child was not? He stresses to these parents that school is part of life's progression and that teaching is like parenting in some ways. He can discover where the child is in a sequence of skills, provide opportunities for next steps, encourage, and affirm progress. He cannot force any child to match the kid at the next table. Nor, he points out, should he silence the student who is already talking until the other students find their voices. The analogy helps parents understand Mr. Wade's thinking when he differentiates instruction throughout the year. He invites parents to help him understand their child's development and interests so that together they can be effective catalysts for growth.

Helping Parents Learn About Differentiated Instruction

As a rule, parents are eager for their children to learn, grow, succeed, and feel valued in school. A differentiated classroom is an ideal place for those things to take place. Share this with your students' parents. Explain that the way a differentiated classroom looks may differ at times from what they may expect, but the goals of that classroom reflect what most parents want for their children.

Helping parents develop a clear understanding of differentiated instruction and how it benefits their children opens the way for you to partner with them to maximize their children's growth. It's useful for parents to understand the following:

• The goal of differentiated instruction is to make certain that everyone grows as much as possible in all key skills and knowledge areas, moving on from their starting points.

• In a differentiated classroom, the teacher closely assesses and monitors skills, knowledge levels, interests, and effective routes to learning for each student, and then plans lessons and tasks with that range of variance in mind.

• When the teacher assigns a differentiated task, it reflects the teacher's current best understanding of what a child needs to grow in understanding and skill. That understanding is evolutionary and will change as the year goes on, as the child grows, and as parents contribute to the understanding.

• The teacher will also give students a great deal of voice and choice in the work they do, with a goal of helping them learn to make consistently wiser choices and assume increasing independence and ownership of their own success as learners.

• The teacher welcomes conversations with parents about their children because both have important perspectives to share. A teacher has a broad view informed by experience with children this age and developmental benchmarks. A parent has a deeper view in regard to the child's interests, feelings, and change over time. When the wide-angle lens and close-up lens both contribute images of the child, the picture becomes fuller for everyone.

A Note About Differentiation and Parents of Advanced Learners

Parents of advanced learners often get labeled as pushy. No doubt some of them are (as are some parents of any group of learners), but for the most part, they just want the right things for their children. They value learning, want their children to do the same, and are eager for a classroom that is challenging and invigorating. Many of these parents have come to distrust school because their children have spent so much time waiting for others to learn what they already knew.

There are several important guidelines for working with parents of highly able students (many of which also apply to most parents).

Listen to them and learn from them. They have a story to tell and want someone to hear it and to be invested in the growth of their child. All parents ought to get that kind of reception in school.

Rebuild their trust that school is a good fit for their child. As they see your investment in tapping into and extending their child's understandings, skills, talents, and interests, you are likely to see skepticism replaced by gratitude.

Understand the paradox of parenting a bright child. Most parents of highly able students want their child challenged. They know that a good piano teacher recognizes musical talent and mentors the student in developing that talent. Most accept that a coach recognizes athletic talent and pushes young people to extend that capacity. So, on one hand, parents of bright learners want these kinds of high expectations in their child's classrooms and this same kind of push. On the other hand, however, they, like their children, may have become comfortable with easy success and may become anxious or unhappy—at least in the short term—when the work actually becomes challenging. While these parents want a challenge for their child, they may also want you to guarantee that the challenge will involve no risk, no stumbling, no failure. Those two desires are incompatible. Risk-free talent development, painless challenge, and growth without tension are anomalies, if they exist at all.

You may have to help some parents come to understand that reality, and in those times, your message ought to be this: "I see the capacity in your child. I am excited about being a part of developing that potential. I can't do that and also promise that everything will be easy and that he will never stumble along the way. I can't promise that As will remain automatic. But I promise you that I will be aware of the struggle and will do everything I can to be a partner with your child in learning to struggle, overcoming obstacles, and ultimately discovering that he has a far greater reach than he thought he did. My goal is not to punish him or to cause him to fail in the long term. To the contrary, I know I will be an effective teacher if I can help him learn to rise to a challenge and to find satisfaction in effort. Will you help me with that?"

Think through the "Why is my child's work harder?" question. If you establish the sort of understanding with parents described in the previous suggestion, you will eliminate many a tense discussion that occurs when a parent is afraid of challenge for their child (even as they seek it). Nonetheless, a parent may ask you why the work their child is doing is "harder" than that of another child in the class.

In a differentiated classroom, a readiness-based assignment needs to be just a little too hard for a student's current proficiency level. That's how human beings learn and grow. The goal of the teacher in a differentiated classroom is to ensure, as often as possible, that each student has to work a little too hard, and to ensure that the student will find a support system that will assist with and support continuing growth.

The real answer for a parent who asks, "Why does my child have to do harder work than someone else?" is that, relative to that child's skills and understanding, the work is no harder than the work of any other child relative to that child's skills and understanding. Much of the discussion must rest on the reality that developing capacity takes struggle—for all humans, even very bright ones. Most students encounter struggle regularly in school. Bright kids must, too, if they are to become all that they can be. The noted children's author Katherine Paterson keeps this reminder above the desk where she writes: "Before the gates of excellence, the high gods have placed sweat" (1981, p. 3). Much as we might wish otherwise, we have no reason to believe she's wrong.

A Note About Parents Who Push Students Too Hard

Probably less common than the parents of bright students who want challenge and ease simultaneously are the parents who push their child to do work that is far too taxing. There is the possibility, of course, that the parents see capability in the student that is there but hidden from view in school. For that reason, it's not a bad idea to let a student try something you believe may be too demanding.

In the life of every teacher, some of the most compelling stories are of students who bloomed when the teacher didn't expect it. On the other hand, there is a difference between expecting *much* of a child and expecting *too much*. If the task does appear to be too difficult for the child, if it causes the child persistent tension and frustration, and if it leads to confusion and self-doubt rather than clarity and self-confidence, it's too much. It's important to help parents understand that learning is impaired when students feel overtaxed, afraid, or out of control. A conversation something like the one described before between Mr. Wade and parents of his students might be helpful.

It is also useful if you can help these students find a voice to express their tension and unhappiness. The message to parents may be clearer from their child than from a teacher. Also, in a situation where parents are unduly controlling, young people often feel mute. Regaining a voice and becoming a self-advocate can be important in helping these students gain a greater sense of power in their own world.

A Note About Parents Who Stay Away from School

There are many reasons why parents stay away from school. In some cases, parental absence may not create a problem for a student. In other cases, however, the parents who stay away are the ones we most need to invite into the child's world at school. Some of these parents stay away because school was alienating for them and returning is too difficult. Some stay away because they do not speak the language spoken in parent conferences, or because their cultural norm is that parents should not try to usurp the role of the teacher. Some stay away because their lives are too burdened to add one more thing. We err as teachers in assuming that these parents don't care about their children's education. That is rare indeed.

Most parents, including those who keep their distance from us, care deeply about their children's schooling and see it as a way for their children to achieve a good life. It is critical that schools and teachers build bridges to these parents, communicating with them in whatever ways we can find—including but not limited to making school a more inviting place for them. They need to hear our messages that we believe in their children and see concrete evidence of this. They need to hear the success stories of their children. They need to receive specific suggestions of things they can do to be strong partners in their children's learning.

We also need to hear from parents so that we can understand better each child's life and culture and language and history and dreams. We need to know the stories that get brought home from school, and the parents' perspective on what will work best in helping their children learn. It is easy for us to assume that everyone's view of the world is like the one we grew up with. That is not the case. Reaching out to every parent in effective ways helps us expand our worldview and become more effective teachers.

Successful partnering between teacher and parents is based on proactive communication. Call a student's home occasionally with positive news about a child. From time to time, send home class newsletters—electronic or print, based on the format most likely to reach parents, and in the parent's primary language when that is feasible. Share goals for specific projects, how various procedures are working in class, and so on. Spotlight a broad range of students in the communications. Ask for parents' reactions and suggestions related to their child's experiences in your class. Work with your school to make school "invitational" for parents, just as you do for students, so that many more parents feel comfortable in joining forces with you to create a classroom in which individuals are known and honored, and in which much is expected from every student.

The next chapter begins our look at the "how to's" of differentiation with a focus on planning for variance in students' readiness levels.

Planning Lessons
Differentiated by Readiness

Three dimensions of student variance guide planning for differentiation: readiness, interest, and learning profile. We know that students learn better if tasks are a close match for their skills and understanding of a topic (readiness), if tasks ignite curiosity or passion in a student (interest), and if students have the freedom to work in a way that is more efficient or that makes learning more accessible for them (learning profile). In this chapter and the next two, we'll take a look at the basics of differentiating instruction in response to those three student traits.

This chapter focuses on readiness differentiation. A task that's a good match for student readiness extends that student's knowledge, understanding, and skills a bit beyond what the student can do independently. A good readiness match pushes the student a little beyond his or her comfort zone and then provides support in bridging the gap between the known and unknown.

Expert teachers often do the equivalent of "playing by ear" when they differentiate instruction in their classrooms based on the readiness levels of their students. That is, they simply do what seems right for their students. Generally, intuition begins the process, and over time teachers learn from their successes and failures in "pitching" materials and tasks at appropriate challenge levels for students' current points of development, refining their understanding of making a match between student readiness and task design. Thus, when we ask teachers how they plan a differentiated lesson in response to student readiness, their answers are often a bit vague: "I just try to match the tasks to the students' readiness level," or "I put them in groups I think will work," or "I give them choices." Clarity about differentiation by readiness can hone and refine teacher instincts, giving the teacher a greater sense of comfort with readiness differentiation and providing students more appropriate learning experiences.

Thinking About Differentiation by Readiness

To successfully differentiate instruction according to student readiness, it helps to have a comprehensive guide for planning and monitoring the effectiveness of differentiated lessons. One way to get specific guidance about what skilled teachers do when they create differentiated lessons is to study those lessons and discover what makes them differentiated. We can also learn much by asking, "What makes this lesson differentiated in response to a student's readiness level?" Figure 9.1 is an answer to that question, derived from looking at many examples of differentiation. The tool in this figure is called "the Equalizer."

Designing differentiated instruction is similar to using the equalizer controls on a piece of sound equipment. There, you achieve the optimal balance for each piece of music by moving sliding levers across several different continuums to boost or cut different sound values: volume, fade, pitch, and so on. In planning for differentiated student work, adjusting the "sliders" appropriately to account for various students' different points of development equalizes their chances of being appropriately challenged by the materials, activities, and products or assessments in your classroom. Let's take a closer look at the range of settings at your disposal.

Foundational to Transformational

When students encounter an idea that is new to them or a skill with which they are not yet proficient, they often need to practice it in a manner that's similar to the way they experienced the idea or skill in class. That is, they may need time to practice applying the idea in a straightforward and familiar way: "I think I see how we did this in class yesterday. Now I'll see if I can use what I learned in an example that's a lot like yesterday's example." In these instances, the materials students use and the tasks they do should be foundational—that is, basic, familiar, and presented in ways

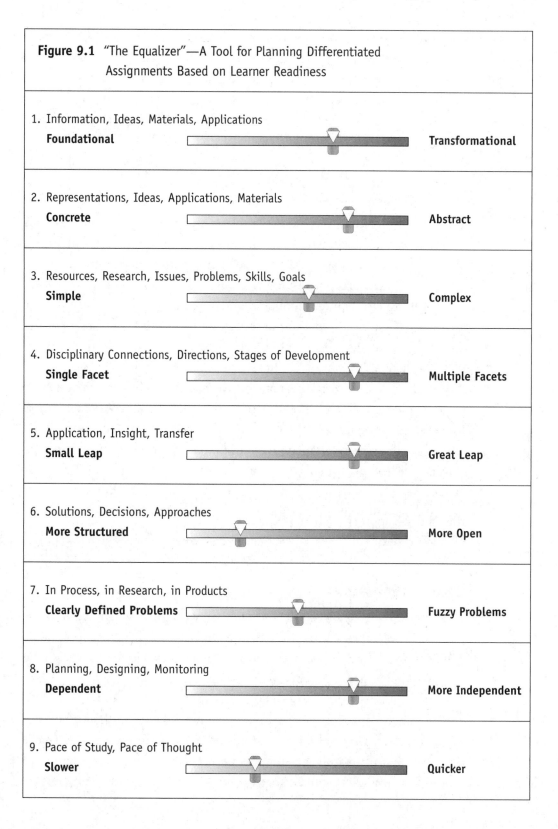

Figure 9.1 "The Equalizer"—A Tool for Planning Differentiated Assignments Based on Learner Readiness

1. Information, Ideas, Materials, Applications
   Foundational ——————————————— **Transformational**

2. Representations, Ideas, Applications, Materials
   Concrete ——————————————— **Abstract**

3. Resources, Research, Issues, Problems, Skills, Goals
   Simple ——————————————— **Complex**

4. Disciplinary Connections, Directions, Stages of Development
   Single Facet ——————————————— **Multiple Facets**

5. Application, Insight, Transfer
   Small Leap ——————————————— **Great Leap**

6. Solutions, Decisions, Approaches
   More Structured ——————————————— **More Open**

7. In Process, in Research, in Products
   Clearly Defined Problems ——————————————— **Fuzzy Problems**

8. Planning, Designing, Monitoring
   Dependent ——————————————— **More Independent**

9. Pace of Study, Pace of Thought
   Slower ——————————————— **Quicker**

that foster a solid foundation of understanding. As ideas or skills become clearer to students, or if these ideas or skills are in a student's strength area, they need challenges that are further the to right along the "foundational to transformational" continuum—ones that ask them to apply these ideas and skills in contexts that are increasingly unlike those encountered in class. They need information that helps them develop more depth about the idea. They need to stretch and bend the idea and see how it interacts with other ideas to create a new thought. Such conditions require materials and tasks that are more transformational.

Let's say, for example, that young learners are studying about animals and how animals' body types are adapted to the environment in which they live. As a whole, the class has examined body coverings of a trout, an eagle, a polar bear, and a porcupine—talking about how the animals' body coverings are well-suited to their environments and developing vocabulary that helps them talk about body covering in terms that a scientist might use. For the initial follow-up task the next day, some students may benefit from a more foundational or familiar task of analyzing and describing body coverings of a whale, a hawk, a grizzly bear, and an armadillo. Other students, whose work gives evidence that they understand both the concept of adaptation and yesterday's analysis of the four animals, need a more transformational task of predicting how changes in environment would likely affect the body covering of several animals over time. In a math class, one young learner may be ready for a basic application of the concept of fractions by arranging pieces of cut fruit to reflect a given fraction. An appropriate challenge for another student may be the more transformational task of proposing a way to divide irregularly shaped objects in half, in quarters, and in fifths.

Concrete to Abstract

Students usually need to become familiar with the key information or material about an area of study before they can successfully look at its implications, meanings, or interrelationships. However, once they grasp the information in a concrete way, it's important that they move on to meanings and implications. Working with concrete information should open a door for meaningful abstraction later on. For example, grasping the idea of plot (more concrete) typically has to precede investigations of theme (more abstract). But ultimately, all students need to delve into the meanings of stories, not just the events. Likewise, it's generally a more concrete task to propose a theme for a fable, where the author often provides strong hints about the "lesson" of the story, than to propose a theme for a poem, which even in its structure is often more abstract and where the theme is generally left to the reader to construct. The issue here is timing—when, but not whether, some students should be guided in abstract thinking while others are not.

Simple to Complex

Sometimes students need to see only the big picture of a topic or area of study—just its "skeleton," without many details. Even many adults would likely find it helpful to read a children's book on black holes, for example, before they tackle the work of Stephen Hawking. When the big picture is needed, students should have resources, research, issues, problems, skills, and goals that help them achieve a basic framework of understanding with accuracy and clarity. On the other hand, when the "skeleton" is clear to them, they'll find it more stimulating to add "muscle, bone, and nerves," moving from simple to more complex.

Some students may need to work more simply with one abstraction at a time; others may be able to handle the complexity of multiple abstractions. For example, some students may be ready to work with the theme in a story (a single abstraction), while other students look at interrelationships between themes and symbols (multiple abstractions, or complexity). Some students may need to develop clarity about how events and conditions in Europe just prior to World War II facilitated Adolf Hitler's rise to power. Other students in the class might be more appropriately challenged by comparing and contrasting conditions and events that led to the rise of several dictators during the time span encompassing World War I and World War II. Students whose early exploration focused only on Hitler's rise to power may benefit from examining conditions that were catalysts for multiple dictators' rise to power later in a unit or later in the school year.

Single Facet to Multiple Facets

Sometimes students are at peak performance when working on problems, projects, or dilemmas that involve only a few steps or solutions to complete. It may be all that some students can handle to make a connection between what they studied in science today and what they studied last week. Those with greater understanding and facility in an area of study are ready for and more challenged by following complicated directions. They are more challenged by solving problems that are multifaceted or require great flexibility of approach, or by being asked to make connections between subjects that scarcely seemed related before. In general, learners fare better with tasks that have fewer parts or requirements as they initially explore and make sense of skills or ideas, and may be more appropriately challenged by working with multifaceted tasks, issues, or problems as their understanding of and facility with the topic grows.

Small Leap to Great Leap

Note that this continuum does not provide the option of "no leap." Students should always have to run ideas through their minds and figure out how to use them. Activities that call only for absorption and regurgitation are generally of little long-term use and in many ways are the enemy of engaged learning.

But for some students, learning something (say, the procedure for measuring area) and then applying that learning (by estimating and verifying the area of the hamster house compared to the area of the teacher's desk) may be enough of a leap of application and transfer, at least in the beginning. Other students in the same class might be able to move from estimating and verifying area to estimating materials needed for a building project and the proportional cost implications of increasing the building area. In both cases, students make mental leaps from reading information on a page to using that information. The latter task calls for relatively greater leaps of application, insight, and transfer, but all of the students are asked to think about and use what they are learning.

Structured to Open-Ended

Sometimes students need to complete tasks that are fairly well laid out for them, so they are guided or coached through a process. They don't have too many decisions to make or unknowns to deal with. Novice drivers begin by managing the car on prescribed driving ranges or delineated routes. Students new to creating computer animations may benefit from using an animation app that presents choices to students and creates an animation based on those choices. In time, many students will enjoy the challenge of creating an animation on a more open-ended and less guided platform. Some will be competent in using a professional animation platform and professional equipment. Likewise, using a paragraph frame for a writing assignment may be greatly helpful to some students as they begin to develop persuasive arguments, whereas other students are comfortable in writing persuasive pieces with no frame at all. A step-by-step guide to a chemistry lab often may be far more sensible than "improvisation" for some students, while other students, with a greater understanding of the purpose of the lab and the knowledge behind it, may be more appropriately challenged by completing a lab where they have to determine and defend the appropriate steps in the lab. At some point in the learning process, structure or modeling helps most of us become confident enough eventually to solo. When modeling has served its purpose for a student, the teacher needs to remove the "training wheels."

Dependent to Independent

Independent study, thought, application, transfer, and creation are goals for all students. But just as some students grow taller sooner than others, some will be ready for greater independence earlier than others. It can be helpful for teachers to think about independence developing across four stages (Tomlinson, 1993):

1. *Skill building*—A time when a student needs to develop the ability to read and follow directions, make simple choices, follow through with short-term tasks, set and monitor goals, use resources appropriately, and so on.

2. *Structured independence*—A time when a student is ready to make choices from teacher-generated options, follow prescribed time lines, draw appropriate information from resources using note-taking guides, engage in self-evaluation according to preset criteria, and so on.

3. *Shared independence*—A time when a student is ready to identify issues or generate problems to be solved, design tasks, find and use resources effectively, set timelines, establish criteria for evaluation, and so on. The teacher helps the student "tighten" or focus the plans and monitors the production process.

4. *Self-guided independence*—A time when a student plans, executes, and evaluates his or her own tasks, seeking help or feedback only when needed. It's likely that only a small number of students, even at the high school and college levels, function well at the self-guided independence stage. For example, doctoral dissertations are generally cast at a level of shared independence. Fully self-guided independence is indicative of

professional-level work, and even there, most individuals benefit from working with mentors or colleagues who can expand their thinking and increase the likelihood of robust outcomes. By guiding students across this continuum at paces that are appropriate for them, you and your students are less likely to become frustrated by tasks that require greater independence than they are currently ready to exercise.

Slow to Fast

Of all the continuums, this one is the most likely to require some "jumping around." There are times when students with great ability in a subject need to move quickly through familiar or minimally challenging material. But at other times, some of those same students will benefit from having more time to work on an assignment than you would allot for students with less facility in the area. Remember, a slower pace can allow for deeper exploration. Likewise, although it's often the case that students who struggle with a task or skill can be quite successful with it if they have more time to complete the task or learn the skill, sometimes it makes great sense to "accelerate" the learning of strugglers by eliminating less critical knowledge and skill on a topic from their learning agendas so that they can focus on the learning that is most likely to propel them forward with maximum competency and power (Hopfenberg & Levin, 1993; Sousa, 2011). Matching pacing to your students' needs is a critical differentiation strategy, and it is a hallmark of a class structured with enough flexibility to support consistent growth for all students in the class.

Readiness Planning Points to Keep in Mind

Just as a sound engineer might need to move just one slider on the sound board to achieve the optimal balance, it's possible for the teacher to design an effective lesson or task for a student by adjusting just one of the factors we've discussed to address that student's particular needs. For example, a student may be a very competent thinker but also be pretty disorganized. That student should be able to handle a complex, abstract, multifaceted task (sliders over toward the right on Figure 9.1) as long as the teacher adjusts the task directions to keep the "independence" slider toward the left— perhaps, for instance, setting more "check-in" dates for that student than is necessary for more self-guided students working on the same assignment.

Achieving the proper balance for a piece of music doesn't generally require moving every single slider, and it's the same when it comes to planning differentiated instruction; you don't need to think about every factor we've discussed for every single task. In addition, it's rarely necessary or wise to shove all the sliders to the far left or far right for a particular student or group of students. In other words, don't err by assuming that a student lacks either strengths or deficits. Plan so that you stretch a student with his or her strong points (sliders more toward the right) and support the student in his or her weaker areas (sliders more toward the left).

Troubleshooting Tips for the Equalizer

When using the heuristic guide in Figure 9.1 to modify lessons for a differentiated classroom, keep in mind three essential caveats.

All students need lessons that are coherent, relevant, powerful, transferable, authentic, and meaningful. We should not consign some students to drill and practice as the staple of their school diets and save the rich and engaging lessons for others.

Curriculum that is good for students pushes them a bit beyond what they find easy or comfortable. Our best teaching happens when we give students a genuine challenge and then help them successfully meet it. Differentiated instruction, implemented effectively, is so powerful because it offers various levels of genuine challenge. Your students' sense of self-efficacy comes from recognizing their power after accomplishing something they first thought was just "too big" for them. Design your lessons to stretch all students beyond their comfort zones in knowledge, insight, thinking, basic skills, production and presentation skills, and affective awareness.

"Teach up" and plan so that you encourage your students to "work up." In other words, *be ready to match students to tasks that will stretch them.* A good task for a given student is one that is just a bit too hard and through which the teacher ensures the presence of support required for success. We err most often as teachers by planning a single task that is "easy enough for most students to complete." This has the effect of establishing "middling" or low expectations for many learners while still setting expectations that are out of reach for some. Challenge is always, always individual. A task is challenging enough for a given student when it causes that student to stand on "mental tiptoes" and reach high to complete it well.

The ideas embodied in the Equalizer get at the heart of what many skilled teachers do when they automatically adapt instruction for varied learner needs. Use it as a guide when differentiating **content** (what you teach and what students learn), **process** (how students think about or make sense of ideas and information), and **product** (how students show what they know). Add other continuums and descriptors to this guide as your students teach you more about how to differentiate instruction.

It is also helpful to think about particular strategies for differentiating instruction in response to student readiness levels. Figure 9.2 suggests a few such strategies.

Figure 9.2 Some Strategies for Addressing Students' Readiness Differences

Apps that support reading, writing, and math development

Brainstorming groups

Compacting

Directions written in simpler language, shorter sentences, with bullets, or with more white space

Flexible use of time and deadlines

Games for practice at student's readiness level

Graphic organizers to guide student work and thought just beyond student's current performance level

Hand signals and other cues

Highlighted texts

Hint folders

Learning contracts, learning menus, personal agendas, Think-Tac-Toes, learning tickets

Opportunity to demonstrate early mastery and work with more advanced assignments

Peer review

Personalized criteria for quality

Personalized feedback

Print and digital text at student's independent reading level

Questions at varied levels of complexity

Reading, writing, and/or math workshops

Recorded readings or texts

Small-group construction

Step-by-step video explanations, directions, or models

Supplementary materials at student's independent reading level

Teacher presentation in multiple modes

Text and/or supplementary materials in a student's home language

Tiered assignments, labs, writing prompts, homework, products, or assessments

Varied reading partnerships

Varied scaffolding for reading, writing, math, technology, independence

Varied ways to express learning (including on assessments)

In using any of the strategies to match student readiness, you are likely to be using materials, tasks, or scaffolding that corresponds to one or more continuums on the Equalizer. For example, if you bookmark various websites for students to use in research and then try to match the difficulty level of the various sites to the skills and understanding levels of various students, you may find that some sites are more concrete and some more abstract, or that some are simpler in vocabulary or ideas while others are more complex.

You might also have all students use the same sites, building a support system to allow success for less-skilled readers (greater dependence) while encouraging skilled readers to work with the sites more independently. Try the combination of strategies and Equalizer continuums in your own classroom.

Using Readiness to Differentiate Content, Process, and Product

Teachers can differentiate any or all of the three key components of curriculum (content, process, and product) in response to student readiness. For example, a French teacher differentiates **content** for her learners by using two French-language websites in a reading and translating task. Students having more difficulty with reading and translating French use the first website, which is designed for students learning French and written with simpler vocabulary, grammar, and syntax. Students more proficient with French translation use a website designed for French-speaking adolescents. The two websites generally contain many articles on the same topics, but the website written for French-speaking adolescents requires more complex skills of translation and comprehension.

A math teacher often differentiates **process** (activities) for her students based on their readiness levels by assigning or offering homework assignments on the same topic at varying degrees of difficulty. She helps students determine which assignment would be most likely to both clarify their thinking and challenge them appropriately.

A middle school teaching team differentiates **product** (performance assignments) based on student readiness in a number of ways. One is by using varying portions of rubrics, or quality indicators, with different students. Each student receives two or three columns of a five-column rubric and works with the teacher to designate his or her goals for the product assignment by circling targets on the rubric. By selecting which columns to provide to which students, the teacher aims to focus each individual on the levels of performance that seem at or above his or her current proficiency and provide a choice of ways to "work up" through the self-selection of goals within each category represented on the rubric. It is nearly always the case that students circle goals in each of the rubric columns and can explain the indicators that represent their current strengths and those that indicate competencies still in the early stages of development.

When teachers use readiness level as a focus for differentiating content, process, and product, their aim is to push students just a bit beyond their particular "comfort zones" so that student work feels just a little too hard. They then support students in stretching to achieve a next level of competency with important skills and ideas.

The next chapter focuses on students' interests: planning to keep a group of diverse individuals engaged in your lessons by linking key ideas and skills in the content with experiences, skills, and ideas that are important in the lives of your students.

10

Planning Lessons Differentiated by Interest

A wise teacher knows the importance of having a plan to "hook" and engage students with the topic at hand. Engagement is a nonnegotiable of teaching and learning. Key motivators for learning are a voice in and choice of topics, work that is personally meaningful, and a feeling of ownership of the task at hand. Tasks that tap into student strengths and build a sense of competence in the learner are also strong motivators. All of these elements are directly related to interest-based differentiation (Bess, 1997; Brandt, 1998; Csikszentmihalyi, 1990; Deci & Ryan, 1985; Williams & Williams, 2011).

• • •

Content, process, and product can all be differentiated according to student interest. For example, Mr. Elkins differentiates **content** in response to student interest during a standards-based unit on reading and writing nonfiction. While there are key understandings and skills on which all his students will focus, he has learned that allowing them to read and write about topics that they find genuinely interesting makes the work of building the required skills and mastering the key principles more engaging. As he has seen firsthand, if a student has a spark of curiosity about a topic (or better still, a fire), it's more likely that student will learn. And so, when the unit begins, he guides students to select reading materials and topics they care about, and he builds the unit around their selections. Students work independently and in small, interest-alike groups some of the time. Other times, they work together as a class to establish foundational understandings, to plan for their independent work, to share what they are learning, to troubleshoot, and to explore ways in which common themes and skills are evident in their varied areas of focus.

•   •   •

Ms. Bell likes to use Jigsaw, a collaborative learning strategy, to differentiate **process** in response to student interest. As she and her students explore a broad topic in science, she asks each student to select a facet of the topic that he or she finds intriguing. At various points in the unit, Ms. Bell creates Jigsaw teams that call on students to explore their areas of special interest with other students who selected the same facet of the topic. They then share what they learn with classmates who explored different facets, so that everyone learns something about every other specialty. Ms. Bell provides discussion guides to help students find and organize information and ideas and engage in meaningful conversation in their Jigsaw groups.

•   •   •

Mrs. Gomez finds differentiating student **products** in response to interest an ideal way to boost engagement. Her approach is to provide rubrics that delineate criteria for success for three or four different kinds of products and allow students to select one of these—or propose a product idea of their own, along with criteria for success. Along the way, as students work on their products, brainstorming groups are used to help generate ideas. They also review one another's work using the rubrics and offer suggestions for strengthening the work. The class as a whole discusses how students are planning for quality work.

A colleague, Mrs. Phan, takes advantage of her school's "maker space," which gives her geometry students room to work alone or in design teams to create products that demonstrate mathematical applications in design contexts. Students' work can be focused on engineering, art, or everyday needs. Mrs. Phan requires that all work demonstrate clear applications to mathematical principles and practices they've shared in class, but she encourages students to involve math beyond the scope of their in-class work. She also uses a periodic modification of a "genius hour" concept to enable students to use some class time to think about geometric and algebraic applications in the world around them and how they might extend or improve on those applications. She finds that the students' persistent focus on uses of mathematics in sports, hobbies, medicine, mechanics, science fiction, and a host of other interest areas makes the content livelier and more compelling to them.

Thinking About Differentiation by Interest

Teachers who care about their students as individuals make it a priority to find out about the interests students bring to the classroom with them, and teachers who care about differentiation find a way to use these insights to inform their planning. Dynamic teachers also try to create new interests in their students. When a teacher is passionate about a topic and shares the passion with his or her classes, similar interests often emerge in some of the learners. A teacher who raises intriguing questions, introduces ideas that make content vibrant, and supports students in learning more about those elements also helps to generate new student interests.

Drawing on Existing Student Interests

The goals of interest-based instruction include (1) helping students realize that there is a match between school and their own desires to learn, (2) demonstrating the interconnectedness of all learning, (3) using skills or ideas familiar to students as a bridge to ideas or skills less familiar to them, (4) helping students develop competency and autonomy as learners, and (5) enhancing student success. When a teacher encourages a student to look at a topic of study through the lens of that student's own interest, all five goals are likely to be achieved.

There are many strategies for drawing on student interests and linking them to the curriculum. Here are three examples.

"Sidebar" Studies

At the beginning of the school year, Mrs. Janes asks her 7th grade history students to list things they like to think and learn about in their own lives. Typically, the topics they mention include music, sports/recreation, people, families, reading, transportation, heroes/villains, medicine, food, travel, humor, clothing, books, unsolved mysteries, cartoons, and teens. She regularly pulls out a list of these topics as she puts together units, and it's no different for an upcoming unit on the U.S. Civil War. She knows that the concepts of culture, conflict, interdependence, and change will play a significant role in the unit; these concepts will guide much of the year's study. She wants students to read and discuss the textbook along with various supplementary and primary source materials. They will also visit a Civil War battlefield, have speakers visit their classroom, and watch videos about the time period.

On the first day of the unit, Mrs. Janes suggests to her 7th graders that they could learn a great deal about the Civil War period by exploring it through their own interests as those interests were manifest during the Civil War. She helps them set up "sidebar" investigations that will continue throughout the unit. Their job, she explains, will be to see what their topic shows them about life during the Civil War in general, and about culture, conflict, change, and interdependence in the United States and the Confederate States from 1861 to 1865. They can work alone or with a partner on these sidebar studies.

To support student success, Mrs. Janes helps everyone develop planning calendars, set goals for their work, and establish criteria for quality. She sets check-in dates to monitor student progress along the way and, as the unit continues, she occasionally conducts minilessons on research for students who want help with information finding. Occasionally students have some designated class time to work on their sidebar investigations, and they also work on their sidebar study during ragged time—when they finish in-class assignments with time to spare. Sometimes sidebar work is homework.

Mrs. Janes finds that concept-focused class discussions throughout the unit are punctuated with insights the students are developing through their sidebar investigations. Students have stories to tell that make the time period come alive for everyone. Motivation is high, and learning is connected both to past units and to students' present-day lives.

Interest Centers or Interest Groups

In Mr. Hernandez's primary classroom, there are always times when students can meet in interest groups. For every topic his students are studying, he creates an interest center to allow his young learners to learn more about what they are curious about. For example, while students are studying animal habitats, there are interest centers on the habitats of various animals such as badgers, beavers, and polar bears. In those centers, students can learn about these particular habitats as a way of expanding the unit's understandings.

Students who want to do so can also form an interest group with one or more peers to create a new interest center focused on a different habitat. When the interest center is complete, it's open for their peers to explore. In these interest groups, students sometimes read together, sometimes have book discussions, and sometimes share what they are finding out from their own research. They plan, design, and do the work necessary to create their new interest center. Meanwhile, the whole class continues its study of habitats.

Mr. Hernandez finds that interest groups that form during units often continue to meet well after the unit ends. His way of combining interest centers and interest groups encourages students to both develop new interests that take hold and expand existing ones in exciting new directions.

Specialty Teams

In an upcoming literature unit, Ms. Bollinger wants her 4th graders to explore ways authors use descriptive language to help readers "see" what they are writing about. There are a number of texts recommended for this kind of language exploration, but she believes her students will be more interested in the work if she allows them to look for effective and varied examples of description in the kinds of writing they most like to read. She sets out her plan. Students will form specialty teams to look at effective description in several kinds of writing: short stories, novels, fantasy, science fiction, nature writing, poetry, lyrics, and action comics. There will be three to four students with a common interest in a particular kind of writing on each team, and she'll provide task guidelines to focus students' search for the elements central to powerful description: use of figures of speech, choice of verbs and adjectives, use of slang or regional language, wordplay, words created by authors, originality, sentence construction, and so on. Students will need to be ready to use what they learn in their specialty teams in a class discussion. As a cumulative activity, each group will decide on passages to nominate for the Descriptive Hall of Fame, present those passages to the class, and defend their choices.

In her presentations, class discussions, peer review groups, rubrics, and so on, Ms. Bollinger is careful to spotlight the elements of literary comprehension and writing mandated in state standards. However, she finds that her students are more engaged in this kind of learning when it is embedded in reading and writing that have real meaning for them, and when the students have a strong voice in determining the contexts in which they will learn about and apply the standards.

Each of these examples shows how existing interests can be a vehicle for learning more about and becoming more invested in important ideas delineated by the curriculum. As these teachers demonstrate, taking an interest-based approach does not mean diverting attention from required understandings and skills; on the contrary, it tends to make this content more accessible, relevant, and memorable to a wider variety of students.

Expanding Student Interests

One of the great pleasures of teaching is the chance to introduce students to a world full of ideas and opportunities. Interest-based instruction not only draws on interests students have but can also help them discover new passions. Once again, there are many approaches available to teachers. Here are a couple of examples.

Real-Life Applications of Ideas and Skills

Ms. Byrd is eager for her students to realize the links between math and the adult world of work. Her 6th graders know little about what most adults do in their daily work—including, she has discovered, what their parents' jobs are like. She has asked each of her students to interview someone whose job or hobby seems interesting to them to find out how that person uses fractions and decimals in their occupation. Students will ask some preliminary questions to determine whether a potential interviewee does, in fact, use fractions and decimals in important ways. If not, a student will continue the search for someone whose job meets both criteria for the assignment: someone who does work that seems interesting and who uses fractions and decimals as an occupational tool. Students observe or shadow their interviewee, if possible.

Ms. Byrd's goal is for students to see that math is central to many kinds of work. She also knows that this exploration will help students develop an increased awareness of and interest in ways people earn a living and make a contribution to society. She and the students develop interview questions and come up with a range of ways in which they can show what they learn. Some requirements are common to all students, including specifications for showing precisely how the person uses fractions and decimals.

Last year, students found out about the usefulness of fractions and decimals in jobs such as anesthesiologist, auto repair technician, media specialist, salesperson, secretary, pilot, pharmacist, composer, and business owner. Ms. Byrd finds that math becomes "new" and exciting as students connect it with new and exciting insights about the world of work. She also thinks the experience will help students think in more focused ways about hobbies they might want to explore or jobs they might like to have someday—and how to prepare for these even at a young age.

New Forms of Expression

Mrs. Landis was tired of seeing the same four or five formats for history projects. Her students, she decided, were "stuck" on posters, dioramas, papers, and timelines as a way of showing what they learned. She invited six adults to visit the class to show alternate ways they expressed ideas—either in their work or related to their avocations. One man presented a captivating performance as a traveling medicine man. Another demonstrated the art of storytelling. A third visitor talked about photojournalism and how students might think about taking pictures to reflect insights about history. A fourth visitor presented ideas through a combination of drama, mime, and music. A fifth visitor talked about her use of a symposium format to communicate. A final visitor demonstrated effective use of websites and apps as vehicles for sharing ideas. Each presenter left the students with descriptors for a quality presentation in his or her particular mode of expression.

Now, with a new unit about to begin, Mrs. Landis sets a challenge for her students: to avoid the "favorite four" ways of expressing their learning and either use one of the new formats their classroom visitors had demonstrated or propose a new option of their own (along with criteria for quality work in that format). Her goal, she explains, is not so much to have the students try something they already knew they were good at, but to persuade them to take a chance on forms of expression that will help them see both themselves and history in a new light.

A Few Guidelines for Interest-Based Differentiation

Interests are, in a way, windows on the world. A developed interest in one area is almost inevitably a route to learning about many other things. It's helpful to think about some interest areas that students may have or might be able to develop. It's also a good idea to extend our own awareness of other ways in which people express their ideas, feelings, and skills. Figure 10.1 provides a beginning framework for considering options you might present to students for interest-based learning. There's much more that could be added to the figure, however. Feel free to expand it as you go.

There's no single recipe for tapping or expanding student interests, but here are a few pointers to consider. They should make interest-based differentiation more effective.

Link interest-based exploration with key components of the curriculum. There's nothing wrong with an opportunity for students to meander about in an area of interest. In general, however, it's wise for the teacher to provide a bit of focus for the interest-based study. It's likely the curriculum specifies certain concepts, categories, understandings, and skills that students should acquire. If the teacher can help students see how those essential curricular elements are revealed through learning about an interest area, then both the student's goals and the goals of the curriculum can be served simultaneously. Further, common class discussions are much easier if all students explore common understandings and use common skills—even though the interest-based explorations differ broadly. That combination allows for both extension of student horizons and reinforcement of required knowledge, skills, and understandings.

Provide structure likely to lead to student success. As there should be, there's an element of student independence required for interest-based differentiation. That's the case because different students will be pursuing different interests, as opposed to everyone in the class moving lockstep through the curriculum. Some students are highly independent, even at an early age. Others need much more guidance to succeed. In every case, it's the job of the teacher to provide the sort of scaffolding that helps a student grow in independence—even those who are already more independent than peers their age. Think about elements such as posing questions for inquiry, setting and pursuing goals, rubrics, timelines, teacher checkpoints, peer critiques of drafts, mini-workshops on conducting research, and other structures you can develop to ensure that your students work smarter in their interest-based efforts.

Develop efficient ways of sharing interest-based findings. It's often not the best use of time for each student in a class of 30 to present their work to every other student. That's particularly true if we've not invested

Figure 10.1 Examples of Potential Student Interests Within a Variety of Categories

Science

Alternative energy sources
Animals
Climate change
Disease
Epidemiology
Forestry
Geology
Meteorology
Oceanography
Research
Wildlife

Social Sciences

Archeology
Anthropology
Mental illness
Psychology

Technology

3–D printing
App development
Digital cartography
Ethical issues
Security
Web design

Theater

Comedy
Costuming
Improvisation
Lighting design
Musicals
Playwriting
Staging

Transportation/Vehicles

Airplanes
Drones
Futuristic vehicles
Helicopters
Motorcycles
Race cars
Submarines

History/Social Studies

Civil Rights movement
Clothing
Demography
Geography
Heroes and villains
Immigration
International issues
Lives of young people
U.S. presidents
Vietnam War

Literature

Biography
Comics
Cultural literature
Fantasy
Graphic novels
Mythology
Poetry

Math

Engineering applications
Geodesic domes
Math games
Math patterns in nature
Research

Modes of Expression

Animation
Blogging
Creative writing
Dance
Debate
Expository writing
Poetry
Visual arts
Website design

Music

Composing
Different genres
Digital music
Directing
Instruments
Singing

Art

Artists
Airbrushing
Cartooning
Graffiti
Jewelry
Museums
Painting
Photography
Sculpture

Collections

Books
Comics
Music
Sports cards
Toys

Community

Access to healthy food
Animal rights
Affordable housing
Conservation
Law enforcement
Political reform
Prison reform
Parks/national parks
Urban design
Voting rights

Competition/Sports

Bodybuilding
Gaming
Individual sports
Music/movie awards
Olympics
Running
Soccer
Street games
Team sports

time in teaching students how to be compelling presenters. Sharing quads, in which each student presents to three others, may be more effective than whole-class sharing. The quads are sometimes most effective when all students in the quad have a common interest. At other times, however, students learn more by sharing with students who explored different interests. You may want to think about having students share interest-based products with adults or other young people who have a similar interest. (In that case, have the student find his or her own audience as part of the product requirements.) Another sharing option that makes for efficient use of time is to have students create online or physical exhibits that others can peruse on their own, rather than have every student report out in an oral presentation.

Create an open invitation for student interests. One way to contribute to an open and inviting classroom environment is to let students know that you welcome their ideas and want them to let you know what they are interested in. When students know they can propose ideas for tasks and projects and believe you'll help them find a way to expand their own interests, there is a much greater sense of shared ownership of learning. Fortunate students hear teachers say, "Here's an idea I had. How can we make it better?" or "Here's something important to learn about. How would you like to come at it?" or "What would make this interesting for you?"

Keep an open eye and an open mind for the student with a serious passion. From time to time, there's a student who is on fire to learn about something that's just not part of the curriculum. You may well be the best teacher for that student if you can find a way to let him or her pursue that passion—even if it means giving up some of what *you* had in mind. For some students, the greatest gift a teacher can give is permission to explore a topic, time to do it, and an interested ear.

Chances are that such a student won't become an academic wreck because he or she misses one class project or a week of homework or some class discussions. Your affirmation that the student's hunger to learn is worthy of nurturing and trust may count for much more in the long run than a carefully prescribed and rigid curriculum. Besides, you can often embed the required agenda in the student's agenda if necessary.

Take full advantage of digital resources—and support students in doing the same. Information on an endless array of topics is available to students, often in multiple languages. New platforms for engaging with information and sharing ideas proliferate at a stunning pace. Technologies that were once available only to professionals or those advanced with avocations are now often accessible not only to a more expanded audience, but also to individuals at varied levels of proficiency with skills and equipment. It's not unusual for students to be proficient with sources and technologies their teachers are unaware of or with which their teachers are less comfortable. Encourage students to take advantage of contemporary resources and technologies to pursue interests and extend expression and sharing of ideas. When teachers can't help students use particular resources or technologies, students can often help one another, if the teacher provides those opportunities. Older students, or students more advanced with a particular resource, can mentor younger or less experienced ones. Students can be encouraged to develop interest-based inquiries with the support of an adult mentor who can guide their work so that it takes advantage of available technologies. Within the bounds of safety and good judgment, the world of knowledge and expression are at the fingertips of students.

Remember that interest-based differentiation can, and often should, be combined with other types of differentiation. It's possible to have a task or product that combines common elements for a whole class, some readiness-based components, some interest-based components, and some learning profile options. Although it's convenient to think about differentiation according to the categories of readiness, interest, and learning profile, it's not necessary to separate the categories in planning or in instruction. It's frequently the case that differentiating simultaneously in two or in all three areas of student variance is natural—and makes really good sense.

Strategies That Support Interest Differentiation

There are many instructional strategies that are ready-made to support interest-based differentiation. Figure 10.2 (see p. 106) lists a number of them. While this book does not afford the opportunity to explore each of the strategies listed in the figure, here is a brief overview of a few of them. You can find more information about all of these strategies in print and online.

Orbitals

This strategy encourages students to raise questions that interest them personally, find answers to their questions, and devise ways to share their

---

Figure 10.2 Some Strategies for Addressing Students' Interests

Access to print and digital resources on a wide range of topics	RAFT assignments
Anchor activities focused on student interests	Specialty groups
	Student-collected vocabulary lists
Design-a-Day options	Student/community mentorships
Designated student experts	Student-developed product and performance task options around essential KUDs
Discussion groups based on student interest in particular aspects of a topic	Student-selected readings
Independent studies	Teacher-generated connections between key content and student experiences/interests used in discussions, lesson design, writing prompts
Interest centers	
Jigsaw	Writing derived from student experiences
Math problems based on student interests	
Orbitals	

---

findings with peers. Because questions can vary in complexity, and the duration of the finding-out process can vary as well, this approach is a way for students with quite different levels of academic or research sophistication to develop interests (Stevenson, 1992).

Design-a-Day

Students decide what to work on for a class period or several class periods. They specify the goals, set the timelines, work toward their goals, and assess their own progress. This strategy is useful when students have a particular interest to pursue or when they'd like to do something they've seen a classmate do during a differentiated class. The strategy is also a good early step in preparing students to succeed with longer and more demanding formats, such as learning contracts.

WebQuests

The WebQuest is a teacher-designed, inquiry-based learning strategy developed with specific learning goals in mind, some specified and relevant Internet links, and guidelines that support students in the research process. The teacher designs a WebQuest to give individuals or small groups of learners the opportunity to use research, problem solving, and basic skills as they move through a process of finding out about, drawing conclusions about, and developing a product on a topic or question. WebQuests can easily be differentiated by readiness, but they are also particularly well suited to differentiation based on student interest (*Education World*, 2013a; Kelly, 2000). See also http://webquest.org/.

Jigsaw

In this collaborative strategy, students work in "expert groups" with peers who study one facet of a topic or unit. They then return to a "home-base" group for sharing what they have learned. Each reconstituted home-base group includes a representative from each of various expert groups. All members of the home-base group are responsible for reporting to the group on their specialty topic and for learning what other students report (Clarke, 1994; *Education World*, 2013c).

Literature Circles

This student-led and role-based discussion format allows students to read on topics of interest and share insights with classmates. It allows teachers a structured and comfortable way to break from the sense that all students must read the same materials in order to have meaningful discussions (Daniels, 2002; *Education World*, 2013b). Literature Circles can also be a highly useful strategy for forming groups at students' readiness/reading levels and forming groups that attend to both reading level and interest simultaneously.

Discussion roles (e.g., Discussion Director, Vocabulary Guru, Fact Checker) are an integral part of Literature Circles. These can be rotated among students so that everyone learns to fill all roles, but the format also allows students to specialize, at least some of the time, in roles that are an especially good fit for them. Role specialization might be linked to student interest or reflect a student's learning profile.

Although Literature Circles are widely associated with English/language arts, the basic format—shared reading based on student interest or readiness followed by student-led discussion governed by clear roles and guidelines—is useful as a differentiation strategy in content areas such as social studies/history and science, and it can easily be adapted to support student inquiry and peer dialogue in art- and math-based conversations and problem solving. In math classes, for example, roles might include Problem Presenter, Questioner/Clarifier, Proposer of Alternate Pathways,

Visual Interpreter, and so on. In social studies/history classes, roles might include Text Summarizer, Vocabulary Expert, Logic Master, Evidence Finder, Questioner/Clarifier, and Presenter of Alternative Perspectives.

Negotiated Criteria

In this strategy, the teacher specifies some whole-class requirements for product or task success and students contribute criteria of their own, which generally reflect their personal interests or priorities. The teacher might also specify one or two criteria for an individual student.

As an example, consider a middle school history class where all students are tasked with citing evidence from multiple texts to build a reasonable argument. The teacher asked Josh, Jalen, and Asia, who are strong readers and thinkers, to use sources that reflect varied perspectives on their topics. Jaden added the personal criterion that the sources be from different time periods. Asia's personal criterion was that she use very precise language in her written argument. Josh elected to develop a new note-taking system to organize this research.

Interest-Based Math Problems

Indications are that when math teachers offer students problems associated with their particular interests (e.g., sports, movies, music), there is an achievement benefit. Students solve problems faster and more accurately, and the strongest gains tend to be for those who were struggling most with standard textbook problems (Walkington, Milan, & Howell, 2014). Putting this strategy into practice is simply a matter of surveying student interests and constructing math problems focused on standard core concepts but with contexts that are relevant to students. "You're selling tickets for a concert" may be of great interest to some, while "You need to estimate the cost of building a new home" or "You are working at a company that develops video games" might appeal more to others. What the students are asked to do in the problems is essentially the same; it's only the situation that varies. It's necessary, of course, to help students learn to identify and transfer the knowledge and skills they use in successfully solving interest-based problems to other contexts, but it's likely that a sense of agency and confidence in using a skill they are less comfortable with in a more familiar and interesting context provides students with an important boost in early learning.

Interactive Notebooks

Interactive notebooks encourage students to think broadly and deeply about a topic and can be teacher-guided, student-directed, or some combination of the two. They allow for use of sketches, organizers, folded pages, flowcharts, pictures, and so on. The flexibility of an interactive notebook makes it a worthy format for an ongoing student investigation of a topic of interest. Providing models of interest-based interactive notebooks for students at levels of complexity appropriate for their current development can introduce ideas for using the notebook in purposeful, thoughtful, and creative ways—as can rubrics that guide the use of interest-based interactive notebooks.

There is increasing conversation in educational circles about the benefits of creating classrooms and schools in which students have voice and ownership. It's easy to argue for schools as places where students come to believe that learning is fulfilling, consuming, and deeply satisfying; it's more difficult to realize this goal. Interest-based differentiation is a step in that direction. Teachers in all classrooms—those with required curricula as well as those with a project focus, an inquiry focus, or the intent to have students design all aspects of their curricula—are wise to understand the connection between students' interests and their motivation to learn.

The next chapter explores ways in which teachers can include students' learning profile needs in instructional planning.

Planning Lessons Differentiated by Learning Profile

Learning profile refers to ways in which we learn best as individuals. Each of us knows some ways of learning that are quite effective for us, and others that slow us down or make learning feel awkward. Common sense, experience, and research suggest to us that when teachers can tap into routes that promote efficient and effective learning for students, results are better. The goals of learning-profile differentiation are to help individual learners understand modes of learning that work best for them, and to offer those options so that each learner finds a good learning fit in the classroom.

Factors That Shape Learning Profile

Learning profile is an umbrella term for four factors that influence how individuals approach learning or process ideas: (1) learning style, (2) intelligence preferences, (3) gender, and (4) culture. Teachers who understand learning profile and how these four factors can overlap and interact with one another to influence a student's attitude toward and engagement in different types of tasks position themselves to plan instruction that will allow as many students as possible to learn more comfortably, efficiently, and effectively.

Learning Style Preferences

"Learning style" refers to environmental or personal factors that may impact the learning process. For instance, some students may generally learn best when they can move around; others need to sit still. Some students enjoy a room with lots to look at, color, and things to touch and try out. Other students appear to function best when the environment is more "spare" because they find a "busy" classroom distracting. Some students need a great deal of light in a room in order to feel comfortable. Other students prefer a darker working space. Some students will learn best through oral modes, others through visual means (which might be further broken down into a preference for images vs. a preference for reading and writing), and others through touch or movement. Many students are perfectly comfortable learning in a variety of modes.

Virtually everyone agrees that people learn in different ways (e.g., Sousa, 2011). Nonetheless, teacher attention to learning styles in the classroom elicits significant concerns from some well-regarded psychologists, neuroscientists, and sociologists. Their criticisms are important to understand:

• Although there are a great many learning styles models, including *physiological* (linked to time of day, movement, sound, and light), *psychological* (including global, analytic, reflective, and impressionistic approaches), and *thinking* (including remembering, feeling, reasoning, and imaginative preferences), to name just a few, there are no agreed-upon parameters for what constitutes a learning style. It is perhaps unwise to build instructional approaches on a concept that isn't sufficiently articulated.

• What teachers know of students' learning styles tends be based on self-reported student surveys that rarely, if ever, have reliability and validity.

• Teachers may label students as being a certain kind of learner (e.g., "She is an auditory learner, and he is a visual learner") when, in fact, nearly all people learn in a variety of ways, depending on task and context. It would be wiser to encourage students to learn in more ways rather than steering them toward one mode or another.

• It's often the case that labeling results in stereotyping of students and groups of students. Labels are best avoided when there are other alternatives.

• There is little strong research indicating that assigning students to tasks by learning style results in improved test scores.

• Educators' descriptions of how they use learning style as an instructional planning tool is out of sync with the way the brain actually works (Coffield, Moseley, Hall, & Ecclestone, 2004; Paschler, McDaniel, Rohrer, & Bjork, 2010; Riener & Willingham, 2010).

There are studies that support the use of learning styles in the classroom (see, for example, Sullivan, 1993), but many of these are older and don't meet current standards for rigorous research. Newer research that supports the efficiency of learning style is limited in both scope and amount (e.g., Lisle, 2006). On the other hand, there are experts who confidently recommend that teachers teach and provide learning opportunities in multiple modes because doing so aligns with how the brain learns and facilitates student learning (e.g., Willis, 2006, 2007). In addition, it may well be that some research pointing to lack of impact on achievement is too limited in scope to understand longer-term benefits of providing options for student learning, such as comfort in the classroom, a sense of voice, and development of agency.

All things considered, however, it seems both inadvisable and unnecessary to survey students with the goal of determining "what type of learning style" a student has and to label a student as a particular type of learner who needs to primarily learn in a particular way. It's easy to avoid those practices, and we should. Later in the chapter, we'll look at a variety of ways students might approach learning that do not run counter to current understandings from psychology and knowledge about the brain, and should make the classroom a better fit for more students.

Intelligence Preferences

"Intelligence preference" refers to the sorts of brain-based predispositions people have for learning. Two theorist/researchers have proposed ways of thinking about intelligence preferences. Howard Gardner (1983, 1993) suggests that we each have varying strengths in combinations of intelligences he calls verbal-linguistic, logical-mathematical, visual-spatial, musical-rhythmic, bodily-kinesthetic, interpersonal, intrapersonal, naturalistic, and existential. Robert Sternberg (1985) suggests that we all have varying strengths in combinations of intelligences he refers to as analytic (schoolhouse intelligence, preference for learning in linear ways often typical of school), practical (contextual intelligence, preference for seeing how and why things work in the world as people actually use them), and creative (problem-solving intelligence, preference for making new connections, innovation). Indications are that when students approach learning in ways that address their intelligence preferences, results are quite positive.

Although the concept of an intelligence preference is both different from and better defined than the concept of learning style, critics of learning style use in the classroom sometimes equate the two and use the two terms interchangeably. A body of more current research on outcomes of using intelligence preferences in the classroom shows positive effects on student achievement for students in a wide range of groups (e.g., Grigorenko & Sternberg, 1997; Sternberg, Torff, & Grigorenko, 1998).

Still, even in the domain of intelligence preferences, it's inadvisable for teachers to use survey instruments that lack reliability and validity in an attempt to identify a student's intelligence preference. Teachers should not work from the assumption that a particular student will learn in the same way at different stages of learning, in different content areas, at different times of day, and across other contexts, and teachers should not label students by intelligence preference.

Culture-Influenced Preferences

Culture shapes how we learn. It can influence whether we see time as fixed and rigid or flexible and fluid, whether we are more effusive or reserved in expressing emotions, whether we learn best in a whole-to-part or a part-to-whole approach, whether we prefer to learn material that's contextual and personal or discrete and impersonal, whether we prefer to work with a group or individually, whether we most value creativity or conformity, whether we are more reflective or more expressive—and many other preferences that can greatly affect learning (e.g., Gay, 2013; Storti, 1999). Although some learning patterns may be more evident in one culture than another, there is huge learning variance within every culture, meaning that teachers should not assume that all or even most learners with a common cultural background will learn in the same way. At the same time, creating classrooms that respect students' culturally influenced learning preferences is likely very important in ensuring that students from nonmajority cultural backgrounds feel welcomed and supported in those classrooms (Gay, 2013; Ladson-Billings, 1995, 2009).

Gender-Influenced Preferences

Gender also influences how we learn (e.g., Gilligan, 1982). As is the case with culture, there are learning patterns within each gender but great variance as well. More males than females might prefer competitive learning, for example, or more females than males might prefer collaboration. However, many males will prefer collaborative learning and many females will prefer competition. Whereas females might tend to process ideas more intuitively and males more logically, those preferences will also vary considerably within a gender, and the numbers will change with time and in response to context. Since gender norms and preferences are culturally constructed and reinforced, it makes sense that some of the same behaviors we think of as culturally influenced can also be influenced by gender—expressiveness versus reserve, for example, or a group orientation versus an individual orientation, or analytic versus creative or practical thinking.

Combined Preferences

Combinations of culture and gender will create unique constellations of learning preferences in individuals. Patterns of learning preference become even more complex when we look at an array of possible combinations of learning styles, intelligence preference, culture-influenced approaches to learning, and gender-influenced preferences. Figure 11.1 presents some continuums of learning preferences that may be shaped by culture and gender. It's important to note that the traits are listed as continuums and to know that individuals would be located along the continuums, not all at one end or the other. Remember, too, that individuals will vary in the degree of an attribute they exhibit at varied times and in varied contexts. What the continuums can do is remind us to honor and provide for students who may work most comfortably with significantly different orientations.

In light of informed criticism of some common classroom practices related to "learning style" and a kaleidoscopic array of variance among individuals in approach to learning, teachers must be thoughtful when considering learning differences and differentiating for them in the classroom. The following guidelines provide some direction.

Figure 11.1 Some Learning Preference Continuums That May Be Shaped
by Culture/Gender

Challenging. . . . . Respectful

Collectivist (group) orientation . . . . Individualist (self) orientation

Competitive . . . . Collaborative

Creative/practical approach. . . . . Analytical approach

Creativity (divergence) . . . . Conformity (convergence)

Emphasis on ideas/abstractions . . . . Emphasis on facts

Emphasis on objects . . . . Emphasis on people

Expressive. . . . . Reserved

Feelings-driven . . . . Information-driven

Flexible sense of time. . . . . Fixed sense of time

Introspective. . . . . External focus

Intuitive processing . . . . Logical processing

Linear/step-by-step approach . . . . Global approach

Need for external structures . . . . Self-structured

Need to test ideas . . . . Need to observe

On-demand response . . . . Reflective response

Social orientation . . . . Achievement orientation

Whole-to-part perspective (general) . . . . Part-to-whole perspective (specific)

Source: Adapted from Dack & Tomlinson, 2015.

Some Guidelines for Defensible Learning-Profile Differentiation

Given the broad agreement that people approach learning in a multiplicity of ways, what's a wise course for a teacher to follow in addressing those differences in instruction? Certainly we must bear in mind both the informed criticism of some common classroom practices related to "learning style" and the kaleidoscopic array of variance in how individuals approach learning. There's no simple approach to this complex challenge, but the guidelines below, and the "Do's and Don'ts" in Figure 11.2, provide some direction.

Help your students understand learning profile differentiation. Explain to students that all people can learn in a variety of ways, and that they are likely to become more effective learners as they expand their

Figure 11.2 Key Do's and Don'ts for Learning Profile Differentiation

DO's	DON'Ts
DO help students understand that people vary in their approaches to learning, depending on what they are trying to learn, when they are trying to learn it, and what the goals for learning are at a given time. Help them learn to make thoughtful choices about how they work.	**DON'T** assume any student has a fixed or singular approach to learning.
DO teach in multiple modes and give students opportunities to learn and express learning in multiple modes.	**DON'T** attempt to classify a student according to any one learning category.
DO think about your own learning preferences and how those influence your instructional plans.	**DON'T** assume that all of your students learn best in the ways that you learn best.
DO gather evidence to help you build a picture of your students' ever-evolving learning profiles.	**DON'T** assign work solely on the basis of a student's learning style, intelligence, preference, gender, or culture. **DON'T** generalize. **DON'T** underestimate the power of readiness and interest differentiation.
DO ask your students about their ideas for how to effectively explore and express learning.	**DON'T** let the mode of exploring or expressing learning trump the KUDs. It's about the knowledge, skills, and ideas, not the cartoon or game board.
DO encourage students to work in less familiar/comfortable modes occasionally to help them expand their range of learning approaches.	**DON'T** be afraid to let students work often in the same mode. They may well be enhancing their strengths.
DO expand the range of options you offer over time for your students to explore and express learning.	**DON'T** take on too much at once. Begin with a comfortable number of learning profile options and grow from there.

repertoire of approaches to learning. Let them know that you work hard to honor many routes to learning and invite them to suggest working alternatives they'd like to see used in the classroom from time to time.

Teach students how to talk about their preferences, and provide varied options for them. Let students know you're offering creative, practical, and analytic learning choices today, or that you've intentionally created both competitive and collaborative study formats for the product they are working on, or that you're making a connection between whole-to-part (global, big idea) and part-to-whole (detail) portions of today's lab. As you explain the options available, be deliberate about your terminology to help them recognize and articulate the approaches they respond to best and enjoy most. Then invite students to talk about which approaches are currently making learning effective for them and alternative approaches they might take when they are feeling "stuck."

Identify your own learning preferences, and remember that some, but not all, of your students share some of these. Recognizing your own patterns can help you be more mindful of the opportunities you create for your students and more aware of when a wider range of options should be available. For example, if you generally prefer listening to learn over reading to learn, you may be prone to be an auditory teacher, as well. That's great for kids who tend to learn in that way, but not great for kids who often learn better when they read or move around to learn. If you were successful in school, you may find analytic and part-to-whole learning a breeze. Some students in your class will gravitate to those approaches as well, but students who need more creative, contextual, or whole-to-part approaches may feel like they are working in a fog unless you stretch your own comfort zone and teaching repertoire to account for other approaches to learning as well.

Be a student of your students. It's not easy to see the world through another person's eyes, especially when that person's life experiences are very different from your own. All too often we fail in this regard when it comes to students whose cultural backgrounds are not like ours.

It's essential to watch individuals in your class for clues about ways in which they access learning. Talk with them about what works and doesn't work for them, and invite them to make suggestions or pose alternatives that seem more promising. It's also useful to ask parents to provide insights into what routes to learning work, or don't work, when their students learn at home. If we can expand our vision beyond the parameters of our own private universe, we become more welcoming and effective teachers of all children.

Select a reasonable number of learning profile categories for emphasis as you begin planning for student variance in this area. Think about the students you teach and choices you feel might be more appealing and effective for them. For example, do you have some students who really benefit from working with peers and others who prefer working alone? Do you have some students who are much more expressive and others who are more reflective? Alternatively, think about a set of categories that make sense to you in the context of the subjects and students you teach. Perhaps you're comfortable using Sternberg's (1985) analytical, creative, and practical categories, or visual, auditory, and kinesthetic options. Begin with what seems wisest and most doable, and grow from there. Be sure to ask your students to provide feedback on what you try and to suggest other options for exploring and expressing learning that could help them and their classmates learn better.

Strategies That Support Learning Profile Differentiation

Figure 11.3 lists a number of learning approaches that are helpful to consider when planning for students' varied learning preferences. Here are brief explanations of just a few that are particularly valuable when creating a classroom that makes room for students who learn in different ways.

Complex Instruction

This is a powerful instructional model that emphasizes teachers studying their students to gauge which intellectual strengths each student brings to the classroom. The teacher then designs high-level, complex learning tasks that draw on the intellectual strengths of each student in a collaborative group. Such tasks are also called "groupworthy" (Cohen & Lotan, 2014) because they are designed to be multidimensional rather than unidimensional—that is, to recognize the broad range of abilities represented in the group and provide more ways for all students to contribute to the success of the group by using their particular skills.

Groupworthy tasks use a broad range of resources that might include images, text in the language of a group member whose first language is not English, manipulatives, models, and so on. Groupworthy tasks always address the big ideas, essential questions, and key concepts and principles that are central to the domain students are investigating. The goal is to empower the broadest range of learners to take in and express important learning in ways that work well for them as individuals and to contribute to group success as they do so.

Figure 11.3 Some Considerations for Addressing Varied Learning Preferences in the Classroom

Options for Working Environments	Options for Learning and Learning Expression
Work alone/work with a small group (for example, providing individual desks and collaborative work spaces)	Visual/auditory/kinesthetic/reading and writing
More sound/less sound (for example, providing earplugs for students distracted by sound)	Analytical, creative, practical
Sit still/move around (for example, using stand-up desks, exercise ball chairs, and squeeze balls for students who concentrate better with movement)	Verbal, logical-mathematical, visual-spatial, bodily-kinesthetic, musical-rhythmic, interpersonal-intrapersonal, naturalist, existentialist
Quicker pace/slower pace (e.g., providing flexible turn-in times)	
"Busy" space/"spare" space (for example, providing portable carrels for students who need "visual white space")	

Strategies to Try	
Complex Instruction	Tri-Mind options (Sternberg intelligences)
Entry points	Fortune Lines
Varied approaches to organizing ideas	RAFT assignments
Demonstrations/modeling	Multimedia teacher and student presentation
Picturing/writing	Barometer (opinion lines)
Illustrating vocabulary	Illustrating lecture notes

Entry Points

This strategy focuses on encouraging students to enter a topic or explore it through a learning preference (Gardner, 1993) for the purpose of making the early experience a good fit and setting the stage for success. Entry point explorations can be narrational (storytelling), quantitative (scientific/mathematical approaches), foundational (beliefs or frameworks of meaning at the core of the topic), aesthetic (sensory, arts-based approaches), or experiential (hands-on, personal opportunities to become involved).

Varied Approaches to Organizing Ideas

It's important that students know how to organize their thinking so they can make sense of ideas, communicate clearly, and retain and retrieve information. Often it's less important which approach to organization a student uses than that they have an organizational approach that works for them. When there's no compelling reason for the entire class to use the same organizational approach, encourage students to select from strategies such as summarizing, flow-charting, concept mapping, storyboarding, or outlining. Of course, you'll have to ensure that all students understand the various options, but once that's accomplished, you'll quickly see some students gravitate to one approach while others make different decisions. Offering the approaches can address multiple learning preferences, even though the goal of organizing information in a meaningful way is central to all the choices.

RAFT Assignments

RAFT assignments present students with a range of thinking or communication prompts focused on the same key ideas and skills in a lesson or unit and give them a chance to take on different roles (where they encounter different perspectives on the topic) and express themselves in different modes. RAFT takes its name from the fact that each prompt asks students to assume a Role, for a specified Audience, expressed in a particular Format, on a key idea or Topic central to the study at hand. RAFTs can also be created to address readiness needs and interests.

Using Learning Profile to Differentiate Content, Process, and Product

As is true for readiness and interest, attending to learning profile provides teachers with a way to differentiate content, process, and product. Here are some examples.

•   •   •

Ms. Lide sometimes differentiates content in ways likely to tap in to student-learning profile. She records key materials (or has others do the recording) so that students with an auditory preference can listen rather than being solely dependent on visual contact with materials. She also uses podcasts that have accompanying scripts related to key content in the same way. In addition, she sometimes uses role-play just after the students have completed reading, asking them to volunteer to act out what they have read. She finds that some learners like this more physical approach to comprehension.

When introducing ideas to her students, Ms. Lide makes sure to use graphic organizers to illustrate how parts of their study fit the big picture of meaning. She also makes certain that she uses visuals to illustrate important vocabulary or concepts she is talking about so that students can both hear about and "see" these ideas.

• • •

In differentiating classroom activities (process), Mr. Larsen uses what he calls Menus for Success. He might, for example, offer students four ways to explore a math concept today. One approach might ask students to use words and pictures to create directions for how to solve the kind of problem that's the focus of the unit. A second approach might provide multiple versions of the problem to practice, with the opportunity to check answers for accuracy as they go along. A third option might entail students investigating how this kind of math problem could be used to solve a real-life dilemma. A fourth approach might ask students to use manipulatives and words to demonstrate how the problem type works. After selecting an option, students then decide whether it would be better for them to work on it alone or with a peer. When Mr. Larsen talks with his students about making wise selections from the Menu for Success in order to support healthy learning, he compares it to selecting healthy food options from a restaurant menu in order to support healthy living.

• • •

When differentiating products in response to student learning profile, Ms. Michaels uses several approaches. Because her goal is to assess student growth in ways that let each individual show how much he or she knows, understands, and can do, Ms. Michaels often uses more than one kind of end-of-unit assessment. She may combine tests and portfolios of student work, for example, which not only lets her work with students on effective test taking but also enables students for whom test taking is difficult or uninspiring to show how much they've learned in a more comfortable format.

When Ms. Michaels creates product assignments, she nearly always provides at least two or three choices for how students can express what they have learned. They might opt to create a museum exhibit that includes models and narratives, for example, or write an essay or dialogue, or create an annotated and illustrated timeline. She also tries to vary research materials to include artifacts, visuals, print and digital materials, interviews, and online resources. She varies working arrangements so students sometimes work alone, sometimes work with peers, and sometimes work in whichever arrangement they prefer. Students are always encouraged to propose other working and expression options.

• • •

As we see here, there are many ways to accommodate students' preferred approaches to learning without limiting or restricting their access to all kinds of different learning experiences depending on content and context. Looking for a good learning fit for a range of students means, at least in part, trying to understand *how* individuals learn and then responding with a range of choices suited to the learners and the work that they are doing.

Bringing the Elements Together

In the early stages of differentiation, it's helpful to think about using student readiness, interest, and learning profile to differentiate content, process, and product. Breaking down the task into elements not only lets us focus on smaller and more manageable pieces of teaching, but can also help us assess the degree to which we are looking broadly or narrowly at addressing students' learning needs.

In the end, however, the goal is to have a flow of differentiation so that much of what we do is a fit for each student much of the time. That means our goal is to bring together the elements we can differentiate and ways we can go about differentiating them so that there is wholeness to what we do.

A teacher whose skills of differentiation are fluid continually asks, "Would students benefit from flexibility in approaching today's learning goals?" When the answer is yes, the teacher seeks alternative avenues to learning for her students, and invites them to join her in that quest. Here's a brief example of an elementary teacher's classroom in which differentiation is pervasive, and making room for different approaches to learning is part of the mix.

• • •

Mrs. Chen and her students are studying explorers and exploration. As she considers reading material for them, she makes sure to find selections with a wide range of readability. Sometimes she and the class will read a piece in common. Sometimes she will assign materials to particular students. Sometimes they will select what to read. In this way, she hopes to take into account common needs of the whole class as well as both reading readiness and interests of individuals. Students also have frequent opportunities to select reading material for themselves.

As she plans activities, Mrs. Chen envisions similar-readiness groups for some tasks and mixed-readiness groups for others. For example, when students are honing their writing skills, they may work with students who have similar goals at that time. On the other hand, when they write scenarios to depict the challenges faced by explorers, she may form groups that include, for example, students who have especially innovative ideas, students with a flair for the dramatic, students who write well, and students who are leaders.

As the unit ends, students will demonstrate their learning in part through "exchanges" between past explorers and modern-day explorers. All students are responsible for demonstrating designated knowledge, understandings, and skills. Mrs. Chen will assign each student a past explorer, and students will select their own contemporary explorer from a teacher-provided list, making this selection based on personal interests, such as science, sports, writing, technology, television, and so on. Students may work alone on their tasks, with one partner, or with a group of three to four students. Individuals and groups then select the format for their explorer exchange. Among the choices are a live symposium or dialogue format, a webpage that compares and contrasts the two explorers, a video recording of a conversation between the two explorers, a set of letters exchanged between the two, and so on.

There's certainly whole-class instruction in Mrs. Chen's room, but chances are that whole-class instruction will be followed by opportunities for students to come to grips with ideas and skills on their own terms. Chances are also good that there is flexibility built into much of what goes on so that each student feels the classroom "belongs" to him or her.

In the next chapter, the focus shifts from the areas of student variance that prompt differentiation (readiness, interest, and learning profile) to the curricular and instructional elements we can differentiate (content, process, and product) in response to students' readiness levels, interests, and approaches to learning.

Differentiating Content

Because students process ideas as they read content, think (or process) while they create products, and conjure ideas for products while they encounter ideas in the materials they use, it is difficult and somewhat unnatural to carve apart the elements of content, process, and product. Nonetheless, thinking about how to differentiate instruction is more manageable when you examine one element at a time. Just proceed with the awareness that these elements are more interconnected than they may appear to be on the page.

Content is the "input" of teaching and learning. It's what we teach and what we want students to learn. There are two ways to think about differentiating content: (1) as adapting *what we teach or want students to learn* or (2) as adapting *how we give students access* to what we teach or want them to learn. For example, if a teacher asks some 3rd grade students to begin work with fractions while their classmates are working hard to master division, the teacher has differentiated *what* the students are learning. Similarly, a teacher may elect to assign some 4th graders spelling words that reflect their current spelling skills (which might range from a 1st grade level all way through a high school level) rather than having all students work with a 4th grade spelling program. On the other hand, *what students learn* stays relatively the same, and *how they access the learning* changes when the teacher encourages advanced students to read a novel more rapidly and with more independence and complex writing prompts while he or she finds additional time for struggling readers to read the same novel and use peer partners to support their reading and writing.

In general, in settings where there are agreed-upon standards or goals, there is a benefit to holding *what* students learn relatively steady while changing how we give access to the content to match student needs. Sometimes, however, it does make sense to also change *what* we teach, depending on student needs. The latter is especially sensible when we are teaching a linear progression of skills, such as spelling or math computation.

Differentiating Content for Student Need

Content can be differentiated in response to a student's readiness level, interests, or learning profile. It can also be differentiated in response to any combination of readiness, interest, and learning profile.

Differentiating content according to readiness means matching the material or information you're asking students to learn to a student's current proficiency in reading and understanding. For example, it is a poor use of time to ask a 5th grader who reads independently at a 9th grade level to do most of her work in a grade-level reading series. It is equally inappropriate to ask a student who currently speaks and understands little English to read independently from a grade-level U.S. history book. One way to approach readiness differentiation of content is to use the Equalizer (see Figure 9.1, p. 85) as a guide, asking yourself if the materials are at an appropriately challenging level of complexity, independence, pacing, and so on for all the students who would be using them, and making adjustments accordingly.

Differentiating content according to interest involves incorporating ideas and materials that build on or extend student interests into the curriculum. Examples would be an English teacher encouraging a budding young comedienne to read or view selections that involve humor during assignments focused on craft and structure analysis, or a history teacher helping a student track down resources to feed his curiosity about the role of Native Americans in the Civil War.

Differentiating content according to learning profile means making sure a student has a way of "coming at" materials and ideas that match his or her preferred approach to learning. For instance, some students may handle a lecture best if the teacher uses images as well as speech—linking visual and auditory learning. Some students will comprehend reading far better if they can read aloud, whereas other students need silence when they read. Reading the science text may be just the ticket to help one student understand the concept of "work," while another student may grasp the idea better by watching a demonstration that uses exemplars of "work" and "not work."

Strategies for Differentiating Content

Here are some strategies for differentiating content. Some of them are useful in differentiating what we need students to learn, and many are useful in differentiating how we ensure appropriate access to what we need students to learn. Most can be used to differentiate content by readiness, interest, and learning profile.

Using Varied Text and Resource Materials

Grade-level texts are often far too simple for some students in a given class and yet too complex for others. Using multiple texts and combining them with a wide variety of other supplementary materials increases your chances of reaching all your students with content that is meaningful to them as individuals. You can develop valuable differentiation resources by building a classroom library from discarded texts of various levels (or requesting that textbook money be used to buy three classroom sets of different books rather than one copy of a single text for everyone), and collecting magazines, newsletters, brochures, and other print materials. The rich array of materials available through the Internet and apps makes it far easier than it once was for a teacher to differentiate materials based on student need.

Other things being equal, advanced learners will usually use advanced resources, but they may occasionally find it helpful, when beginning a complex study, to find out about a topic in the more straightforward presentation a less challenging source provides. Likewise, struggling learners may from time to time grasp an idea better by looking at diagrams, pictures, or figures and charts in a more advanced source.

As students' task needs vary, so should their use of resources. Computer programs in math, literacy, and other areas present increasing levels of challenge and complexity. In math or science, some students may need to use manipulatives to understand a concept, while others can move directly from an explanation or reading to abstract use of that concept without working with manipulatives. Some videos present the fundamentals of a topic with clarity, and others provide greater breadth or depth of coverage to extend exploration. For students learning English, it may be useful to read about new concepts in their home language first, then in English. The key is to match the levels of complexity, abstractness, depth, breadth, and so forth of the resource materials with the student's learning needs. Don't forget that a range of text and resource materials can also help you respond to a student's interests as well as his or her readiness or learning profile.

Using Learning Contracts

Learning contracts between teachers and students come in several varieties, including learning menus, learning agendas, and Think-Tac-Toes. Most formats share a basic assumption: given the expectation that they will do responsible and effective work and be provided the necessary structures to support that work, students will rise to the challenge and enjoy a greater degree of freedom in their use of class time. Contracts can contain both skill and content components, and they are well suited to a differentiated classroom because the components and terms of a contract can vary with a student's needs.

For example, students in a 4th grade class are all using contracts. Javy's contract specifies that during contract time in the week ahead he must complete his next two spelling lists, master two levels on the computer program on division by one digit, and work with the characterization project from a novel of his choosing. Javy's spelling lists are a bit above grade level, reflecting his comfort as a speller. Because his math work is below grade level, extra time with the computer or in small-group instruction and practice may help him move along more confidently. The novel Javy selects can be based on his interests, and his task—thinking and writing about himself in comparison to the main character—has been designed to help him use key writing strategies to build characters.

Sofia's learning contract also includes spelling, computer math, and a novel. Rather than a spelling list, she uses an advanced vocabulary strategy because she spells several years above grade level. She will use the computer program to practice division by three digits. She will also select a novel that she likes, analyze the main character, and create an opposite or mirror image character by applying traits of characterization.

Javy, Sofia, the two other friends who share their table, and the rest of their classmates map out their plan of action for the week, decide which tasks will be done in school and which at home, and progress at a rate and depth of content challenging for them. All students are accountable for their time and self-management, and they understand that their teacher will assign them work if they violate their contract obligations.

Learning contracts are a great strategy for a differentiated classroom because they combine a sense of shared goals with individual appropriateness and an independent work format. When students are engaged in contract work, the teacher has time for conferences and small-group or individual work sessions based on progress and needs.

Providing Minilessons

When a teacher introduces a concept to the whole class, chances are that some students will grasp it instantly and be ready to move on to application right away. Others, however, require a little more time—or even a lot more time—to make sense of the "input" the teacher has given them. In such cases, minilessons are a valuable way to differentiate content.

Based on persistent formative assessment of student understanding, the teacher may reteach one subgroup of students using a different approach than the one initially used, meet with another subgroup to extend their understanding and skill, and assemble still another subgroup to review content they missed during absences over the last few days. Minilessons can be quite effective in targeting content to students' interests and learning profiles as well as to their readiness.

Presenting in Different Modes

There's a time in most instructional cycles when teacher presentation makes sense. When planning these portions of your lessons, consider ways in which you might best capture your students' attention and make the ideas you share more memorable and relevant. Perhaps you could integrate sound (e.g., the voices of others, sounds that make a term or concept clearer, music), pictures, stories, charts or figures, models, photographs, artwork, body language, movement (for you and your students), and other elements that involve the senses and engage the mind. Think about creating a podcast or a video podcast of the lecture or presentation so that students who need to hear ideas more than once can have that opportunity. Look to podcasts and videos created by experts outside the classroom to provide some students with additional opportunity to master concepts and others the opportunity to extend or enrich learning. Use interactive whiteboards to help students observe ideas in the making and to access resources that will expand their understanding. Use wikis, blogs, class websites, and social media as tools to help students access ideas and information. Have students act out ideas as they are understanding them, or engage in "in character" first-person exchanges between individuals who see topics and issues through different lenses. All in all, providing students with a chance to access content in different ways generally makes content clearer to more students and learning more durable for all.

Providing Varied Support Systems

You can make content of varying complexity levels more accessible to your students by using a variety of support systems, including apps that introduce skills, apps and websites that provide text at different levels of reading complexity, reading partners, audio and video recordings, and peer and adult mentors. Incorporate these strategies to help many students stretch as learners.

Reading Partners and Recordings

A 5th grader can record books for younger students who would benefit from listening. An advanced 3rd grade reader who records a grade-level book can help create enriching materials for a classmate who has trouble decoding or reading long passages. High school students can make recordings summarizing complex texts on a particular topic to give advanced 6th graders access to materials beyond the scope of their classroom or school library. Some of those 6th graders can help 4th graders learn how to make a speech by making a video or creating an animation on the subject. An advanced 4th grader can make a video about the types of buildings in the community, which could then be used in a kindergarten learning center.

Note-taking Organizers

Some students, even those at higher grade levels, find it difficult to read text or listen to a lecture and come away with a coherent sense of what it was all about. For such students, it can be quite useful to work with a prepared visual organizer that follows the flow of ideas from the text, resource materials, or a lecture. Such organizers can bring forward key ideas and information and also help some learners see how a teacher or author develops a line of thought. Bear in mind, however, that students who read independently may find mandatory use of such organizers restrictive. The point is always to provide individual learners with a support system that helps them grow; supports that keep them "marching in place" or lead them to work below their current performance level are better discarded.

Highlighted Print Materials

A teacher can highlight critical passages in text or supplementary materials, keeping several copies of the highlighted materials at a designated spot that is discreetly accessible to students. When a student has difficulty managing an entire chapter or article, a highlighted version that draws focus to the material that merits the closest attention will be available. From the outside, the material looks like everyone else's—the same novel, the same article—but the highlighting means the student can expend energy on reading and understanding essential portions of the chapter rather than becoming discouraged with what seems like (and often is) an insurmountable amount of print.

Digests of Key Ideas

Most effective teachers could, with minimal expenditure of time, create a one- or two-page capsule of the ideas covered in a unit or textbook chapter. Such a digest can be of great assistance to students who struggle with print materials, lectures, or even organization of information. The digest might be set up as sentences and paragraphs, a flow chart or concept map of the unit or topic, illustrations, or a combination of these. It might also spotlight key vocabulary and provide essential questions the unit is designed to address. Note that the process of creating these digests can help teachers clarify their own thinking about the core of a unit or topic.

Peer and Adult Mentors

Adults often volunteer to help youngsters who are behind with their work and in need of additional guidance. All learners—not just those who are struggling—benefit from time with adults who can answer questions about shared interests, sharpen their thinking, or give them access to advanced research skills. A bright 5th grader can also be a great mentor for an advanced 3rd grader who shares similar interests. You can create extensive support systems by using the people and technologies in your classroom, school, and community, thus giving everyone a chance to reach higher, learn more, and contribute to one another's learning.

Content Differentiation: Two Scenarios

Students in Ms. Jarvis's middle school science class are beginning work on the characteristics of mammals. The unit she's planned features several approaches for introducing her students to key concepts, terms, and ideas about mammals.

First, students select which of five mammals they'd like to investigate (differentiation of content based on student interest). Then, each investigation team can choose one of several ways to learn about their selected mammal. For each mammal, there is a small box of books at varied reading levels (differentiation by readiness). There are also audio and video recordings about each mammal and bookmarked websites (differentiation according to student-learning profile). Further, Ms. Jarvis explains, students can take "freelance" notes on their reading, or use a matrix she's created to guide their note taking (differentiation in response to student readiness).

This is an example of a teacher who is differentiating content in several ways. She is holding steady the key concepts, ideas, and skills (what she wants her students to learn) and modifying how she ensures effective access to the "input" she has defined as essential.

•   •   •

Mr. Okira asks his middle school math students to begin learning about Fibonacci numbers through an introductory investigation. All students must answer the question, "What's the big deal about Fibonacci numbers?" They all have to be able to explain what the sequence is, how it works, and why so many people care so much about it. Ultimately, they will all contribute to a class video on Fibonacci numbers, which they'll present to younger students, but the video creation will come after the introductory inquiry and whole-class study.

Students begin by selecting from nine possible topic categories: animals, flowers, objects in nature, space, weather, architecture, art, music, or geometry (content differentiated by student interest). Once students have chosen the topic that appeals to them, Mr. Okira assigns them to small inquiry groups, based on both their interest and learning strengths (differentiation of content based on learning profile). His goal is to create heterogeneous groups in which each student will have a significant contribution to make to the group. He considers, for example, who is well organized, who approaches ideas creatively, who is a strong oral or silent reader or presenter, who is a strong questioner, a strong illustrator, a strong group builder, and so on. Then he creates teams that can approach the work from varied strengths. Mr. Okira reminds students often of the varied abilities that go into high-quality work and encourages them to use their strengths to help the group do high-quality work. He also provides each group with a "hint card" on how they might begin to find resources that address their topic and how they might best process what they find to answer the required questions. He establishes a schedule by which students can expect him to visit their groups to coach them in their work (hint cards and coaching schedule focus on differentiation of content by readiness).

No doubt you have ways to match the content you teach to learner readiness, interest, and learning profile that work well for you and your students. The goal when differentiating content is to offer approaches to "input" (information, ideas, and skills) that meet students individually where they are and vigorously support their forward progress. The next chapter provides ideas for using varied approaches to students processing in the learning cycle.

Differentiating Process

When students encounter new ideas, information, or skills, they must have time to run this input through their own filters of meaning. As they try to analyze, apply, question, or solve a problem using the material, they have to make sense of it before it becomes "theirs." This sense-making—or processing—is an essential component of instruction. Without it, students either lose the ideas or confuse them.

In the language of school, "process" is often spoken of as an activity. It's probably wiser to use the term "sense-making activity" to remind ourselves that an activity achieves maximum power as a vehicle for learning only when it is squarely focused on a portion of something essential that students need to know, understand, and be able to do as a result of a particular study. For example, students who already understand how to convert fractions into decimals don't need to do an activity designed to help them make sense of the underlying principles; they have already processed and made sense of those ideas. Students who are foggy about fractions aren't ready to benefit from a sense-making activity on converting fractions into decimals; first, they need an activity that will help them clarify the conceptual notion of whole and part that is the underpinning of fractions.

Any effective activity is essentially a sense-making process, designed to help a student progress from a current point of understanding to a more complex level of understanding. Students process and make sense of ideas and information most easily when teachers ensure that classroom activities

- Are interesting to students.
- Call on students to think at a high level.
- Require students to use key knowledge, skills, and understandings (KUDs) and to grasp how these elements are connected.

Good differentiated activities are, first and foremost, *good* activities—ones that have the characteristics noted above. What makes them differentiated is that the teacher offers more than one way for students to make sense of what's important. In fact, a helpful way to think about the relationship between a good activity and a good differentiated activity is this:

A GOOD ACTIVITY is something students will make or do
. . . using an essential skill(s) and essential information
. . . in order to understand, extend, or apply an essential idea or principle or answer an essential question.

A GOOD DIFFERENTIATED ACTIVITY is something students will make or do
. . . in a range of modes, at varied degrees of sophistication, and in varying time spans
. . . with varied amounts of teacher or peer support (scaffolding)
. . . using an essential skill(s) and essential information
. . . in order to understand, extend, or apply an essential idea or principle or answer an essential question.

Differentiating Process for Student Needs

As is the case with content, process (sense-making) can be differentiated in response to student readiness, interest, and learning profile.

Differentiating process according to readiness means matching the complexity of a task, materials, and support to a student's current level of knowledge, understanding, and skill. For example, when providing students with guidelines for writing a persuasive essay, a teacher might distribute three different versions of directions, using ongoing assessment information to match each student with the version best suited to the current state of his or her persuasive writing skills. Some students receive an annotated template on which they can write their initial draft, other students receive a checklist of attributes that they can use to monitor or review their initial draft, and still others receive a checklist of attributes featuring items that are more sophisticated in language and expectations.

Differentiating process according to interest means giving students choices about which facet of a topic they wish to specialize in or helping them link a personal interest to a sense-making goal. During a high school government unit examining how the U.S. Constitution has evolved over time, for example, students might opt to explore how the Constitution and associated laws have defined the rights of women, of African Americans, of young people, or of another group of their choosing.

Differentiating process according to learning profile generally means encouraging students to make sense of an idea via a way of learning that they prefer. They might, for example, explore mathematical patterns through movement or drawing, decide to work on a project alone versus with a partner, or sit on the floor to do work rather than sitting in a straight chair.

Strategies That Support Differentiated Processing

Providing sense-making activities matched to students' needs while keeping all students moving forward is very challenging to do in whole-class instruction. That's where strategies that involve having students work in small groups or independently (see Figure 13.1, page 136) are a big help. Although it's both useful and fun to become comfortable with a wide range of instructional strategies that invite flexible grouping, like those in the figure, it's crucial to remember that what matters most is the quality and focus of what students are doing.

The following are just some of the scores of strategies educators have developed that invite more flexible and responsive sense-making: learning logs, journals, blogs, wikis, graphic organizers, learning centers, interest centers or interest groups, learning contracts, Literature Circles, RAFT assignments, discussion circles, role-playing, cooperative controversy (in which students argue both sides of an issue), choice boards, Jigsaw, Think-Pair-Share, model making, and labs. Tiered assignments—that is, parallel tasks at different levels of difficulty—are particularly powerful vehicles for differentiating process in response to student readiness.

Different instructional strategies engage students in different thinking or processing responses, and sense-making activities are most effective for students when the thinking or processing responses they are called on to

Figure 13.1 Some Ways to Differentiate Process

Based on Readiness	Based on Interest	Based on Learning Profile
Apps for skills practice at varied levels of complexity	Anchor activities keyed to student interests	Analytical, practical, and creative prompts and tasks
Class discussions featuring questions at varied levels of complexity	Apps for enriching a current study based on aspects of the topic of interest to a student	Assessments with varied ways to express learning
Complex Instruction		Assignments with varied ways to express ideas
Consistent plans to extend the learning of advanced students	Class discussions with connections to student interests	Choice of working arrangements
Help stations or help folders	Cubing	Class discussions featuring practical, analytical, and creative questions
Learning contracts	"Genius Hour" approaches	
Peer partners/peer tutoring	Independent studies	Collaborative and competitive learning options
Personalized formative feedback	Interactive journals	Fortune Lines
Print and digital resources at varied levels of complexity	Jigsaw	Hand signals for student communication/participation
Print and digital resources in a student's home language	Learning contracts	Interactive Journals
RAFT assignments	"Let's Make a Deal" assignment and product option (student-proposed, but focused on essential KUDs)	Learning contracts
Small-group instruction	Maker spaces	Manipulatives and models
Think Dots	Orbitals	RAFT assignments
Think-Pair-Share & "buzz" groups	RAFT assignments	Role play/Meeting of the Minds
Tiered assignments, homework, and assessments	Specialty groups	
Wait time		

make match both their learning needs and the specified learning goals. In other words, to accommodate the varied approaches to learning that are a feature of academically diverse classrooms, you'll want to rotate regularly through a wide repertoire of instructional strategies, choosing ones that make sense for the students you teach and the content you're trying to help them learn.

Process Differentiation: Two Scenarios

Students in Mr. Jackson's 2nd grade class are studying communities. Right now, they are examining ways in which animal communities are like and unlike human communities. Last week, students viewed a video about ants. Yesterday, they read about bees and then individually selected one other animal to learn about from a list Mr. Jackson provided. Today, as they proceed with their study, Mr. Jackson makes sure his students understand the elements of a community and how these might apply to animals. To help his students think about and make sense of these ideas, he uses cubing, a reflective strategy with roots in writing instruction, which combines student choice with a little bit of chance. At the center of the activity are physical cubes—six-sided and in different colors, with a direction written on each face: "Describe," "Compare," "Tell your feelings about," "Tell the parts of," "Use," and "Tell the good and bad things about."

Mr. Jackson assigns each student to a table. Some tables are stocked with a blue cube and others with a green cube. Students at blue cube tables are working at or below grade level in reading and writing in class and on formative assessment tasks. Here are the blue cube tasks:

1. Describe an ant community in pictures or words.
2. Compare an ant community to your community in pictures or words.
3. List words that tell your feelings about watching an ant community.
4. Describe the parts of an ant community and what goes on in each part by using words, by using pictures, or by building it.
5. Describe a way that an ant community helps you understand living and working together in a community.
6. List the good and bad things about an ant community.

Students at green cube tables are performing above or well above grade level in reading and writing in class and on formative assessment tasks. Here are the green cube tasks:

1. Describe an ant community using at least three sentences with at least three describing words in each sentence.

2. Use a Venn diagram to compare an ant community with the community of the animal you selected.

3. Pretend that ants think like people (which they don't, of course). Create a comic strip or panel that tells what you think about what an ant feels like as it goes through a day in its community. Do the same thing with another kind of animal from a different sort of community.

4. Make a diagram of an animal community with parts labeled and tell what each part is for.

5. Write a rule for living together in a community and tell how it would be useful in two different communities.

6. Write a song or poem or draw a picture that tells what you think is best and worst about being part of a community.

Students begin by sitting at their assigned table and taking turns rolling the cube. Each student gets two rolls; if the first roll turns up a task the student doesn't want to do, a second roll is allowed—but no more. Students can help one another with tasks and discuss their work together, although each must write or draw his or her own response. When all the tasks are complete, Mr. Jackson rearranges the seating so that all students who did the same task (e.g., Green Cube Task #3, Blue Cube Task #4) can share their varied ideas and approaches.

Blue cube tasks help learners think in a variety of ways about how key elements of community apply to a single animal community. Green cube tasks help learners make such connections among several animal communities. Compared to the blue cube tasks, green cube tasks are more transformational, complex, and multifaceted, and they require greater leaps of insight and transfer on the Equalizer. Later in the unit, students who completed blue cube tasks will complete some of the green cube tasks either in small groups or by working directly with Mr. Jackson. Thus, all students engage in idea and information processing activities that not only match their current needs but also coax them forward on multiple learning continuums.

* * *

Mrs. Miller's 6th graders are all reading the novel *Tuck Everlasting*. She knows that the book is difficult for some of her students and doesn't stretch others much, but she likes to have the class read a book together periodically, just as she often finds it useful to have her students read several different novels simultaneously. Because the current novel is not a "best fit" for all learners in her class, she is making a special effort to use a differentiated process strategy and vary it based on student readiness and interest. Her strategy of choice is interactive journals—giving students writing prompts and calling on them to, for example, predict what will occur next, reflect on something that has just taken place, apply understandings about elements of literature such as conflict or figurative language, relate to a character or situation, and grapple with meanings central to the author's purposes in writing the book.

Whereas once Mrs. Miller would have given all students the same interactive journal prompt every day, this year she is working hard to craft a differentiated classroom, so her approach is a little different. Some days all students respond to the same prompt, because it's essential that they all think about a common idea; other days, her prompts are tailored to her students' different interests and needs. She has also provided students with a variety of examples of ways they can use their interactive journals to respond in ways other than "regular writing"—by creating charts, flip pages, storyboards, and so on.

On the day before students begin reading the novel, Mrs. Miller asks them to open their journals and jot down what they think the word "everlasting" means. After class, she reads these responses. Factoring this pre-assessment data into her cumulative knowledge about her students, the next day Mrs. Miller assigns each student to one of three different journal prompts.

Students who seem unfamiliar with the word work in pairs to complete the following tasks, then record individual responses in their journals:

1. Guess what "everlasting" means and write your "best guess" explanation.

2. Find definitions of the word in two dictionaries and use what you learn from the dictionary to write a good 6th grade definition of the word.

3. Write a definition of "everlasting" that would be crystal clear to a 1st grader.

4. Illustrate at least five things that you believe are everlasting and defend why you think so.

5. Hypothesize what a book called *Tuck Everlasting* might be about.

Students who seem to already understand the word "everlasting" well enough and whose general vocabulary and comprehension are within the expected range for 6th graders respond to this set of prompts in their journals—either working alone or after first discussing the prompts with a partner:

1. Hypothesize what a book called *Tuck Everlasting* might be about and explain how you came to this hypothesis.

2. Present and defend your choices of what sorts of things would be included as everlasting in a book written about everlasting things in your own lifetimes.

3. Present and defend your choices of what sorts of things would be included as everlasting in a book written about life 200 years ago.

4. Present and defend your choices of what sorts of things would be included as everlasting in a book written about life 200 years into the future.

Finally, a small group of students with advanced skills in vocabulary, writing, and abstraction work together as a group to do the following:

1. Place the following list of items—plus additional items of their choosing—on a continuum of "less enduring" to "more enduring": gold, coal, love, friendship, energy, time, fear, and happiness.

2. Write a poem or paragraph or create an annotated visual that expresses the reasoning behind the items' placement on the continuum.

3. Hypothesize what a book called *Tuck Everlasting* might be about and be ready to defend this hypothesis.

All students in the class use interactive journals and have a task designed to kick-start consideration of and insight into a powerful and central concept in the book they are about to begin reading. The processes required to complete the three interactive journal assignments, when plotted on the Equalizer, move from foundational to transformational and from concrete to abstract.

On this day, Mrs. Miller accommodates her students' varied pacing needs by distributing their journal assignment sheets, instructing students to read at least the first 25 pages of the novel, and then letting them be free to work as long as necessary in class on the interactive journal prompt; the work can be completed at home that night, she explains. This attention to pacing allows each student to work at a comfortable pace; ensures that all students have adequate, purposeful work to do during the class period;

and offers enough time so that all of the students should be prepared for a short, whole-class discussion at the beginning of class the following day.

Sense-making strategies help students process and "own" ideas and information in ways that work best for them. The next chapter, on differentiating products, describes strategies that allow students to demonstrate what they know, understand, and can do as a result of all that processing—again, in ways that help each of them move forward as much as possible from their varied entry points.

Differentiating Products

Before we begin looking at differentiating student products, it's useful to distinguish between three related but different mechanisms through which students can demonstrate what they are learning: (1) sense-making activities, (2) performance tasks, and (3) products.

Sense-making activities ask students to make, do, or write something that gives evidence of what they have learned as a result of a relatively brief segment of work—often one or two class periods. Sense-making activities are formative. That is, they occur during spans of practice and, therefore, should generally not be graded, although they do provide excellent opportunities to give students feedback that will help them move forward from their current levels of knowledge, understanding, and skill. Sense-making activities may ask students to demonstrate mastery of specified content or the application of that content.

Performance tasks (sometimes called performance assessments) generally ask students to demonstrate their current proficiency with more extended segments of learning than do sense-making activities. They are often completed at the midpoint of a marking period, at the ends of chapters or units, or at the end of key components of a unit, and they are designed to see how well students can apply or transfer what they have learned so far. Most performance tasks are completed in class within a specified length of time. They are summative in nature and, therefore, generally graded.

Products, like performance tasks, are completed at the end of significant spans of learning—most often at the end of units of study, marking periods, or even semesters. Like performance tasks, products ask students to demonstrate proficiency with essential knowledge, understanding, and skills, and to apply and transfer what they have learned to a context beyond those encountered in class. Also like performance tasks, they are summative in nature and are therefore graded. Products differ from performance tasks in that they are generally more open in terms of supporting student interest and voice, require more time for completion, call on students to work at broader and deeper levels than performance tasks, and often require students to devote time both in and out of class to their development. While performance tasks certainly can be differentiated (*in any way except alteration of the learning goals the task is designed to assess*), the openness and duration of products likely invite greater attention to student readiness, interest, and approaches to learning. Students can work on products alone, in pairs, or in teams. In the latter two options, it's important for the product assignment to include provisions for both individual and group accountability for all essential KUDs.

Products are important not only because they represent your students' extensive knowledge, skills, and understandings—as well as the applications and transfer of those KUDs—but also because they are the element of the curriculum that students can most directly and fully "own." Students need to experience the reality that what they learn in school transcends the confines of classroom walls, the borders of worksheets, and the bubble sheets of standardized tests. They need to see ideas and skills having utility in the broader world. One of the most significant draws of product assignments, then, is the opportunity they give students to do work that feels significant and important and has ties to real life. They are often created to be shared with a meaningful audience.

Well-designed product assignments can be highly motivating. They ask students to give evidence of and extend critical learning while allowing them to apply this learning to personal interest areas and work in preferred approaches. In other words, they allow for differentiation.

Finally, and perhaps obviously, high-quality product assignments also provide excellent ways to assess student knowledge, understanding, and skill. Many students can show what they know far better in a product than on a written test. Therefore, in a differentiated classroom, teachers may replace some summative tests with rich product assignments, or use a combination of summative tests, performance tasks, and summative product options so that the broadest range of students have the maximum opportunity to think about, apply, and demonstrate what they have learned.

We'll take a look first at the elements of effectively developed product assignments. Then, throughout the chapter, we'll look at ways in which teachers might elect to differentiate those product assignments based on student readiness, interest, and learning profile. As is the case with differentiating content and process, the idea is to begin with clear goals in mind—clear and specified KUDs—and create work that will focus student attention on these goals. Then, it's wise to consider ways in which an assignment might support variance in student **readiness** (e.g., complexity of resources, coaching from peers or teacher, sophistication of models provided, access to support in a student's first language, opportunities for in-process feedback, range of complexity in rubrics), student **interest** (e.g., choice of topics through which a student explores or applies essential KUDs, student-generated criteria for success that support expanded learning in an interest area), and **learning profile** (e.g., working alone or with a team; opting to take an analytical, practical, or creative approach to a topic; choice of mode of expressing knowledge, ideas, and skills).

Creating High-Quality Product Assignments

It's important to remember that in order to provide good *differentiated* curriculum and instruction—whether we are talking about content, process, or product—you should first have good curriculum and instruction. Let's take some time to cover the essential guidelines for developing high-quality product assignments, which are an important element in powerful curriculum and instruction.

Identify the key knowledge, understandings, and skills the product will incorporate. A teacher crafts a top-rate product assignment with thought and care, and with explicit reference to the knowledge, understandings, and skills students work to develop over a particular learning span. As noted, a good product is not just something students do for enjoyment to wrap up a unit or semester; it must cause students to think about, apply, transform, and even expand on the identified KUDs.

Decide on the format(s) that product will take. Sometimes the product format is a given, shaped by the requirements of a curriculum (e.g., writing a persuasive essay, designing an experiment, and so on). Often, however, product format offers teachers a way to entice students into enthusiastic pursuit and application of ideas and skills. You might hook young adolescents on poetry, for example, by asking them to assemble photographs that capture the meaning, tone, or themes of a selected group of poems, or get students interested in the application of geometric principles with a product that focuses on interior design. Sometimes a teacher can use a product assignment as a way to help students explore modes of expression that are unfamiliar (e.g., creating a virtual museum exhibit, conducting a symposium, developing a journal article to communicate results of a science investigation).

The very best product formats tend to be those that align with students' enthusiasms (e.g., a 3rd grader with significant musical talent writes a musical to share information and understandings about the westward movement in the United States). For this reason, it's often useful to decide on two or three product options and differentiate further by inviting students to suggest alternative options that are of particular personal interest. In these cases, stipulate that any alternative option requires teacher approval; students should be prepared to explain to you the ways in which their work would effectively address required criteria for success as well as, perhaps, note any additional criteria they would like to include in the mix.

Determine baseline expectations for quality. It's important to clarify what students should pursue in regard to the content in their products, how they should work on their products, and what indicators of quality they should work toward. Later in the process, students might add to and help you modify these requirements to address their individual readiness, interests, and learning needs, but in most classrooms, it is the teacher's job to specify up front (1) the essential knowledge, understanding, and skills that must be demonstrated in student work, (2) the fundamental expectations for quality work, and (3) the essential working conditions (e.g., how resources will be used, how evidence of revision will be presented, how the timeline is set up). As noted, students can certainly contribute to and extend the baseline expectations that will be held steady for all, but most students learn to work in a craftsmanlike way—by following guidelines that are clearly expressed and effectively supported, whether teacher- or student-generated.

A product assignment's baseline expectations should nearly always include the requirement that students demonstrate their ability to apply or transfer key (and specified) knowledge, understanding, and skills. They might (or might not) specify a certain mode of expression—a multimedia presentation, for example, or an essay accompanied by charts that display data appropriately, or a plan for an experiment. Baseline expectations may (or may not) include the stipulation that all students will use both primary and secondary resources as the foundation for their work, or that they will interview at least three experts on a topic. It's wise to provide some way to track the positive evolution of the product; you can do this by requiring students to submit drafts at various stages.

Remember, the baseline expectations for each product assignment should be shaped by the nature of content, the developmental stages of the learners, and the intent of the product assignment itself. Thus, what may be a core expectation in Mr. Daniels's American History product assignment may not be one in Mr. Jeffers's World History product assignment—or even in Ms. Leondra's American History product assignment. Nearly always, however, such assignments should make clear what knowledge, understanding, and skills the product calls on students to use.

Determine support structures. Because a product assignment should stretch students and be challenging, you need to determine ways in which you can support students' efforts so that their hard work leads ultimately to success rather than overdoses of confusion and ambiguity. Options include arranging times for brainstorming ideas to launch the product, for workshops on conducting research or synthesizing findings, for setting and assessing personal product goals, for peer consultation and editing, for actual product design, and so on. Some students may benefit from the support afforded by these and other structural options; others will not need them. The goal is to anticipate what will be necessary to lift a student's sights and build bridges to attaining worthy goals.

Present the assignment. Finally, after this prep work, it's time to present the product assignment—in writing, orally, via video or audio recording, with icons, through models, or with some combination of these to support student readiness or learning profile needs. This is when you share the KUDs and the baseline expectations for quality. This is also when you explain the space students will have to explore individual interests, modes of working, personal quality goals, and so on. The trick is to balance the structure necessary to focus and guide students with the freedom necessary to support innovation and thought.

Differentiate the product assignment. At this point, it's time to present ways in which the product assignment is or can be differentiated to support and challenge each student—time to present your thoughts about the options students have and to work with individuals to adapt the product's baseline requirements according to readiness, interest, and learning profile. Some teachers like to have a "let's make a deal" product choice through which students can propose alternatives to the teacher's design, as long as the alternative leads students to grapple with and use key information, understanding, and skills that are at the essence of the assignment's purpose. Products are a great place to blend and balance teacher ideas for differentiation with a student's own ideas about what will work best to provide the right level of challenge and support.

As a final note, it's tremendously helpful to coach for quality throughout the entire product development time span. Invite students to talk about their ideas, progress, glitches, ways of solving problems, and so on. Share your own excitement about their ideas. Reiterate and clarify what quality means. Talk about how successful people work. Build a sense of personal ownership of work as well as group appreciation of the varied approaches and ideas of members of the group.

Figure 14.1 (see page 148) summarizes components of effective high-quality product design, including the differentiation component.

Other Guidelines for Successful Product Assignments

Here are a few additional guidelines to maximize the power of product assignments and build for student success:

1. Use products as one way to help your students see the ideas and skills they study in school being used in the world by real people to address real issues or problems.

2. Talk with your students often about the need for both critical and creative thinking in their product work. Help them develop thinking skills and build a passion for ideas they are pursuing.

Figure 14.1 Steps in Designing a High-Quality Product Assignment

---

1. **Identify essential KUDs for the unit of study:**
   K (knowledge—facts)
   U (understandings—big ideas)
   D (skills—basic skills, skills of the discipline, skills of production, thinking skills, etc.)

2. **Identify one or more formats or "packaging options" for the product:**
   Required by the curriculum (e.g., essay, experiment, graphing, perspective drawing)
   Hook
   Exploratory
   Talent- or passion-driven

3. **Determine fundamental expectations for quality work in . . .**
   Content (KUDs)
   Process (planning, goal setting, meeting timelines, supporting a position, scope and use of resources, securing and using feedback, editing, etc.)
   Product (size, construction, durability, parts, evidence of quality, etc.)

4. **Decide on scaffolding necessary for student success, such as . . .**
   Idea brainstorming
   Rubrics/criteria for success
   Planning/goal-setting templates
   Storyboards for elements of the product
   Timelines and check-in dates
   Data-gathering organizers
   Formative product reviews/critiques
   Revision/editing guideline/in-process feedback

5. **Develop a product assignment that clearly says to the student . . .**
   "Your product must show you know, understand, and can do the following things . . ."
   "Your product must demonstrate that you've worked in the following ways . . ."
   "Your product must reach the following standards for quality . . ."

6. **Differentiate the assignment as needed, based on . . .**
   Readiness considerations, which include complexity of resources, materials in a student's first language or in auditory format vs. written format, models of work at a student's challenge level, brainstorming groups, assignments crafted to extend a student's current level of independence, templates or other guides to support note taking, intermediate peer and/ or teacher feedback, larger fonts, more white space in directions, and more or less complex language in directions.

   Interest considerations, which include student choice of topic though which to investigate or apply required KUDs, options to work with experts in topic of interest, student-generated criteria to reflect qualities important in the selected topic/discipline, feedback from an expert in the topic/discipline to extend student's reach, use of expert groups to encourage collaboration with peers who have similar interests, and designing products that call on multiple areas of interest to encourage collaboration among students with varied interests.

Learning profile considerations, which include student choice of mode of expression, working alone or with a partner, providing whole-to-part explanations, providing think-time before producing, providing choices for collaboration and competition, and providing both structured and flexible work spaces.

7. Encourage students to propose any of the following that are permissible within the foundational product parameters:
Alternative formats/packaging options
Additional personalized criteria for success
Collaboration, oversight, or review by mentors
Alternative timelines
Alternative audiences

8. Coach for success in all aspects of the product.
Remember: It's the teacher's job to make explicit that which he or she assumes to be implicit.

3. Require that your students use and synthesize or blend multiple sources of information in developing their products.

4. Stress planning and use check-in dates as needed to match students' levels of independence. Use timelines to ensure that students actually use the entire block of time allotted to the project (rather than waiting three weeks and five days into a month-long product span before beginning to work on the product). Zap procrastination!

5. Support your students' use of varied modes of expression, materials, and technologies.

6. Be sure to help your students learn required production skills, not just necessary content. Don't permit them, for example, to do a debate, teach a class, or develop a website without giving them, or ensuring that they find, clear guidance on what quality would look like in each of those formats.

7. Communicate with parents regarding timelines, requirements, rationale for the product, how they can help, and what they should avoid doing during creation of the product. For example, it can be helpful for parents to listen and ask questions as their child develops ideas for the product; it is not helpful for parents to do actual work on the product, to "rescue" a child who waits too long to begin working on the product, or to impose their own topic preferences on a child.

8. Remember that there are many ways people can express themselves. Help students get out of the poster/report rut of products. Figure 14.2 lists just some of the possibilities they might consider for product formats.

Figure 14.2 Examples of Possible Product Formats

Build a planetarium

Choreograph and present a dance

Collect and analyze samples

Conduct a debate

Conduct a series of interviews

Conduct an ethnography

Create a "better" treaty

Create a comic book or zine

Create a dictionary of topic-related terminology

Create a graphic novel or a nonfiction text

Create a memorial

Create a photo essay

Create a series of newscasts

Create a series of political cartoons

Create a series of wall hangings or murals

Create a wiki

Create an art exhibit or portfolio

Create and present a podcast

Create and present a series of monologues

Create and share an interpretive multimedia presentation

Create authentic recipes

Design a game

Design a new product

Design a simulation

Design a website

Design an app

Design and build something

Design and conduct a series of experiments

Design and create needlework

Design and present a puppet show

Design and set up learning centers

Design musical instruments

Develop a solution to a community or world problem

Develop a virtual museum exhibit

Develop an advertising campaign

Develop and maintain a blog site

Develop and present a mime routine

Develop and present a series of public service announcements

Develop tools

Develop, distribute, and present the results of a survey

Draw a set of blueprints

Formulate and defend a theory

Generate a set of explanatory charts or graphs

Generate an annotated multimedia resource list on a topic

Generate, circulate, and present a petition

Make and carry out a plan

Make a resource list

Make a working model

Make costumes that accurately portray a time or characters

Organize and synthesize information from a series of StoryCorps recordings

Plan a journey or an odyssey

Plan and teach a class

Present a mock trial

Produce a set of YouTube videos

Tell a story or recount an event in graffiti art

Write a biography

Write a children's book

Write a collection of poems

Write a new law and a plan for its passage

Write and record a series of songs

Write and stage a musical

Write and stage a play

Write and submit articles to a blog, newspaper, magazine, or journal

Write letters to the editor

9. Use formative (during the project) and summative (after the project) peer and self-evaluation based on the agreed-upon criteria for content and production.

10. Whenever possible, arrange for student products to be viewed by someone other than just you. Many product options can and should lend themselves to real audiences.

11. Consider how students will present their products. Having every student share with the whole class can be very time-consuming—and even uninspiring, unless you've taught students how to be high-quality presenters. As meaningful alternatives to whole-class presentations, consider exhibits, sharing groups of four, and individual presentations to key adults who serve as mentors or audiences.

Product Differentiation: Two Scenarios

Mrs. Appleton's kindergartners have been studying neighborhoods and communities. As a final product, they are going to research, design, and build a portion of their town, showing its neighborhoods and communities. The whole class is working as a group to create and share the final model, which will be quite large. The class will make some decisions and do some tasks as a whole, such as deciding the basic contents of the model and making "blank buildings" that will be turned into representations of actual buildings later.

Students will select other facets of the work based on their interests. Everyone selects one community member to interview as a way of gathering data, some students have opted to make signs for buildings, and each student selects a neighborhood to work on in the model.

Mrs. Appleton will assign some tasks to draw on and extend each student's strengths. Students more skilled with measuring will measure and draw building dimensions. Students with strong fine-motor skills will cut some of the complex pieces; others who are not so skilled in that area will assemble some of the larger pieces of the model. Mrs. Appleton will ask students who are already reading to share additional information with the class. Students who are writing will help make signs.

She carefully designed this project to ensure that all students do both self-selected and teacher-selected (readiness-based) tasks. Mrs. Appleton also makes sure that some tasks require students to work collegially, while other tasks require independent work.

• • •

Students in Mr. Garcia's Spanish II class are working on language and culture projects. A goal for all his students is to gain a deeper understanding of how elements of a given culture interrelate and form a distinct "personality" or tradition of a people. Many students will explore the culture of a Spanish-speaking country by writing travel guides, making videos, creating documentaries, or developing wikis. They will investigate history, religion, economics, celebrations, geography, foods, education, climate, literature, art, and language structure in the Spanish-speaking country they've selected and demonstrate how those elements are interrelated.

Although students have a number of product requirements laid out for them, they will add some of their own criteria for success. They also can choose whether to work alone or in a small group, which mode of expression they will use, which cultural elements they will focus on, and which research resources they will use.

Three students in Mr. Garcia's class are quite advanced in their grasp of Spanish. Language is a high-talent area for them, and two of them speak Spanish as their first language. Mr. Garcia wants these three students to work with the same concepts as the other students in the class but to stretch their thinking. He will differentiate their product assignment based on readiness and ask them to do cross-cultural comparisons. They will examine elements of language and culture across at least three language groups other than Spanish, none of which can be a modern Romance language. The options he's presented to them are Swahili, Farsi, Chinese, Japanese, Hebrew, and Russian. These advanced students have a bit more freedom in designing their final products and the processes for reaching their final destinations. And like the other students in the class, they can also select whether to work alone or with peers and the form through which they will express their learning.

Differentiating Products for Struggling Learners

We often expect far too little of struggling learners. Product assignments are a great place to stretch our expectations for these students and help them develop confidence as learners and producers. Here are some suggestions for ensuring that students who have difficulty with school tasks have both challenging products to create and support systems that will allow them to produce successful, high-quality work.

1. Be sure the product assignments require struggling learners to apply and extend all the essential understandings and skills for the unit or learning period in question. If applicable, integrate the skills and other goals from students' IEPs into relevant, interesting, and meaning-rich product assignments.

2. Use product formats that allow struggling learners to express themselves in ways other than written language alone.

3. Give struggling learners product assignments in smaller increments, allowing them to complete one portion of a product before introducing another.

4. Think about using audio or video directions so struggling learners can revisit explanations as needed.

5. Prepare, or help students prepare, timelines for product work so that tasks seem more manageable or more comfortably structured.

6. Deliver minilessons or miniworkshops on particular product skills such as taking notes in research, conducting interviews, drawing conclusions, editing, and so on. Many students will benefit from this kind of focused instruction—not just those who struggle academically.

7. Help struggling learners find appropriate resources by setting up interviews, bookmarking Internet sites, creating special book boxes or shelves of readable sources on related topics, creating recorded summaries of key ideas and information, and enlisting media specialists to work with students at established times.

8. Provide templates or organizers that can guide struggling learners through each step of doing research.

9. From time to time, review the big picture of the product with struggling learners, asking them to reflect on why it's important, what they are learning, how parts of the product fit together to make a big picture of meaning, how the product relates to what's going on in class, and so on.

10. Whenever it's clear that students are finding product tasks daunting, meet with them as individuals or groups in an ad hoc, advisory capacity, or set up meetings at pre-established times for consultation, coaching, and guidance.

11. Work with struggling learners to target portions of rubrics that reflect their individual needs, focusing them on goals that seem particularly challenging and worthwhile in this development.

12. Help struggling learners analyze models of effective products from prior years to hone their sense of the product's key components, build the language skills necessary to talk and think about the product's elements, and give them concrete illustrations of what good work looks like. Any student models you share should be a bit aspirational but not out of range. You want to "teach up," not discourage.

13. When students do not have resources and support for product completion outside of school, provide time, materials, and partnership at school—before or after school hours, during class, during released time from class, at lunch, or even on weekends. It's important for every student to have an adult support system that expresses belief in the student's capabilities and invests in making this belief a reality.

14. When students speak a primary language other than English, be sure they have access to information in their first language or a strong support system for translating. Also, think about including a stage in the product timeline to allow these students to express ideas in their primary language first and then translate them (with appropriate assistance) into English.

Differentiating Product Assignments for Advanced Learners

The primary concern when it comes to product assignments is ensuring that they require all students to stretch their information base, understanding, thought processes, planning and production skills, and self-awareness. The product assignments that provide the right degree of genuine challenge for many students often fall short of this mark for students who are highly able in a given subject. For these learners, focus on moving the Equalizer's sliders (see Figure 9.1, p. 85) toward the right. Here are a few principles useful for adapting product assignments for advanced learners.

1. Be sure to structure product assignments for advanced learners so they're being stretched forward on a number of the learning continuums—complexity, independence, transformation, abstractness, multifaceted solutions, or great leaps of insight.

2. Consider having advanced learners study the key issues or questions across time periods, disciplines, or cultures.

3. As much as possible, include advanced-level research, such as advanced materials, multiple materials, materials from several media, primary sources, original documents, and student-conducted original research.

4. Consider letting advanced students begin their projects earlier than other students if the complexity of their products warrants this, or direct them to work on their products during ragged time or instead of the standard homework assignment, if they have already mastered the assignment's concepts and would not benefit from further practice.

5. Whenever possible, have each advanced learner work on products with a mentor—someone who works professionally or avocationally with the topic being explored.

6. Let each advanced learner help you develop criteria for expert-level content and production. Work together to determine issues that experts would feel must be dealt with in the product exploration, ways in which those issues should be dealt with, and procedures and standards for production that would be important to an expert. Use these as benchmarks for student planning and assessment.

7. When it would be helpful to do so, arrange to have advanced learners' products assessed by an expert in the field on which the product is based. In some instances, expert assessment is most helpful at a *formative* (in-process) stage of work so that the student can clarify and extend ideas prior to completion of the product. In other instances, *summative* (end-stage assessment) by an expert is useful for advanced learners who want to test their product against genuine high standards. Frankly, we teachers often lack some of the knowledge and skills that a professional in a particular field possesses. Helping advanced learners gain access to those skills and understandings is an important way of ensuring that they stretch their capacity instead being rewarded for "doing what comes naturally."

Final Thoughts on Differentiating Products for All Learners

There are many ways to design, support, and assess challenging product assignments. Just remember to provide written guidelines so students have adequate structure, challenge, clarity of purpose, and expectations for foundational requirements. Remember, too, that beyond those foundational specifications, it's important to leave as much voice and choice as possible in the student's court.

Differentiating product assignments in an academically diverse classroom is beneficial for several reasons. If all products relate to the same key information and understandings, then all students can share in conversations among individuals, small groups, and the whole class. This can occur even as students work in ways that address their *own* readiness levels, interests, and learning modes. By offering variations on well-designed products with core commonalities, teachers encourage all students to draw on their personal interests and strengths. In these ways, all students can grow from appropriate challenges. At the same time, the teacher retains focus on those curricular components he or she deems essential to all learners.

The next chapter takes a close look at grading, with a focus on student performance and parent involvement.

15

Grading in a Differentiated Classroom

By now, it should be clear that in a differentiated classroom, students often work at different paces and with different support systems. While in most schools, students are currently expected to work toward mastery of the same learning standards, two important features of a differentiated classroom are (1) students' right to "begin where they are" in working with the elements of a standard and (2) the expectation that students will grow as learners from their varied starting points. But charting and acknowledging the academic growth of individual students in a differentiated classroom can create a dilemma for teachers whose schools still use a traditional report card and grading system that acknowledge neither of those features.

On one hand, the public expects "normed" report cards. On the other hand, ample evidence indicates that traditional grading practices often do not communicate or motivate as we would like to believe they do. While traditional grading is part of a history that some educators, parents, and students are hesitant to give up, it's plagued by imprecision and confusion about purposes and meaning (Guskey & Bailey, 2010; O'Connor, 2009; Ornstein & Thompson, 1984; Tomlinson & Moon, 2013).

There's little doubt that we can create reporting systems that communicate more clearly to parents and other stakeholders, represent student learning status in a more meaningful way, and play a much stronger role in tapping student motivation to learn (versus their motivation to "get the grades" or to avoid punishment).

Grading in Context

An exasperated teacher once said that her state seemed to have three religions: Baptist, football, and grades. Her implication, of course, was that these things were sacred and not to be tampered with. The revered denomination or sport might change from place to place, but many educators find that grading is one of the untouchables where they live—and that it has a disproportionate influence within schools. It's the tail that wags the dog. It becomes the reason we can't do _____ (fill in the blank).

This is sad, and in some cases, tragic. It means our teaching philosophies and instructional practices are too often shaped by grading systems rather than the other way around. It means teachers try to teach too many students who experience learning in a state of fear, too many who are convinced that school is about racking up high grade point averages rather than about learning, and too many who see themselves perennially assigned to the murky middle—students who are not great and not awful but not noteworthy.

We can do better than that.

We should feel compelled to do better than that.

An important step toward grading that mirrors good pedagogy rather than constrains it and that supports rather than detracts from learning is realizing that grading is one small part of a much larger chain of assessment practices. If we consistently engaged in assessment practices that reflect our best knowledge of teaching and learning, positive grading practices would likely follow.

Here is what experts in assessment and grading (e.g., O'Connor, 2009, 2016; Wiggins, 1998; Wiliam, 2011) advise.

1. Teachers should do less grading of student work. Learning is difficult—especially if our goal is to stretch each learner regularly. Students need time to practice what they are trying to learn, safely and without judgment; we should provide that time. A good analogy is a sports team that practices for an upcoming game for a number of days in advance of the game. Practices aren't graded or scored. Instead, the coaches observe, provide some practice for the team as a whole, ensure that individual players practice in ways that will benefit them as individual players and benefit the team, and provide focused feedback to individuals and the team. During classroom practice time, teachers should engage in formative (ungraded) assessment and provide feedback that guides students to improve their "game." On game day (test day), there will be a score that counts, but until then, it's all about practice and improvement. This one simple change would greatly benefit learning for virtually all students in appropriately differentiated classes.

2. Grading should be based on clearly articulated learning goals that are known to students and aligned with instruction and with assessments. Too often, grading is a "gotcha" game in which students spend an inordinate amount of time trying to figure out what they're supposed to know on a test. Where there is shared clarity about learning goals (called KUDs in this model of differentiation) and these goals are the clear focus of instruction and of formative and summative assessment, success is in reach for far more students. That statement is not an affirmation of "teaching to the test." Students should be learning meaningful ideas with the expectation that they will be able to apply and transfer what they are learning—not just memorize something and be able to repeat it on test day.

3. Grades should be criterion based, not norm based. We should report on student proficiency with designated competencies, goals, or standards, not on their status relative to one another. In the former system, success is a possibility for many; in the latter, it's possible for only a few.

4. Grades should not be clouded by "grade fog." That is, grades should never incorporate factors that obscure what the grade actually represents. Grade fog happens when a student gets points deducted from a test grade because she forgot to put her name on the test paper. It happens when a student does poorly on a test and does an extra credit worksheet to make up points. It happens when a student who otherwise has an A average is given a zero for failing to turn in one paper, which brings his average for the marking period down to a *D*. It happens when an English language learner understands the contents of the science unit but can't write her answer in a paragraph, which is the only expression option provided on the test.

5. When it's time for report cards, use 3-P grading. In the process of 3-P grading (see Tomlinson & Moon, 2013), the teacher tracks and reports a student's performance (status on specified goals/standards/objectives), process (habits of mind and work), and progress (growth on the specified goals) separately. Reflecting student progress toward reaching standards or goals is valuable in helping students and parents focus on growth rather than only on "outcomes." It's important for advanced learners who can currently receive a steady stream of top grades without the kind of stretching that should occur regularly for them in schools. It's important for the many students who struggle in school for one reason or another and who would likely be more motivated to persevere with the challenges of learning if growth were a consideration. Reflecting a student's process, or habits of mind and work, is valuable because it encourages teachers to help all students develop agency as learners by helping them develop the attitudes and practices of productive learning. Grading that accounts for all three *Ps* (performance, process, product) sets the stage for developing growth mindsets in students, teachers, and parents. It makes clear that wise and hard work leads to growth that will ultimately enable students to attain and often surpass expected outcomes. When grading systems value the development of all three of these critical elements, it's much more likely that classrooms and homes will value and support their development as well. (Note that performance, process, and progress grades should not be averaged together. Doing so reintroduces ambiguity about what the single grade really represents and reduces the power of distinct process and progress indicators.)

Additional Approaches to Grading That Support Learning

Standards-based grading indicates the degree of mastery a student has demonstrated at specified points in time on delineated standards or goals that have been designated as central to a content area. Such systems place the focus on competencies, making it much clearer to students and parents where a student is succeeding or not yet succeeding. They also make it possible to generate a grade that focuses precisely on performance. Further, standards-based grading leaves open the opportunity to report on process and progress as separate but critically important factors in student learning.

Portfolio-type assessment and reporting focuses on actual samples of student performance and provides guidance for interpreting this work in light of the goals the work was designed to help students achieve. Portfolios can also be effective in reflecting student growth, habits of mind and work, and standards- or goal-based outcomes. They have particular clarity and power when combined with student-led conferences, in which the learners themselves interpret their work for parents in ways that clarify performance, process, and progress.

These alternative approaches are necessary due to the simple truth that our traditional and ingrained approaches to grading fail too many students. As Earl (2003) reflects, the unspoken effect of grades is particularly devastating for highly able students and those who struggle in school: "For some students, the certainty of praise and success in school has become a drug; they continually need more. For many other students, year upon year of 'not good enough' has eroded their intellectual self-confidence and resulted in a kind of mind-numbing malaise" (p. 15). It is difficult to break this cycle via instruction, as differentiation is designed to do, when grading systems reinforce it continually and powerfully. We need classrooms that respond to learners as individuals, and grading and reporting systems that reflect and support this mission.

Handling Concerns of Advanced Learners and Their Parents

When moving to instructional and grading systems set up to let students "compete only against themselves," the students most likely to encounter initial difficulty are advanced learners who are unused to having to work hard over a sustained time in order to get good grades. Sometimes it takes a while for these students to develop habits of mind and work that enable them to accept and embrace that kind of challenge that will extend their abilities. It's wise for teachers to help both students and parents understand the value of teaching children to "reach high" and the patience and resilience necessary to do so.

The first time advanced learners meet failure—or anything other than predictable success—can be a devastating hit to their self-esteem and self-image. Unfortunately, many don't encounter a real challenge until they take an advanced high school course or get to college. Often, they respond by removing themselves from the situation in frustration and fear. When they do try to meet the challenge, they frequently find they have no sense of how to study or how to monitor and improve their own effectiveness as problem solvers. For these and several other reasons, teachers do advanced learners a real favor by helping them encounter and face challenges earlier in their school career, when there is less at stake in terms of grade point averages and futures. Most important, learning to face challenges at a younger age gives these students more time to develop the planning, self-evaluation, and study skills they need to maximize their potential as learners.

If advanced students and their parents panic at the onset of challenge, you can be a voice of calm and reason. Encourage parents to work with you in helping their children extend themselves to reach for challenge rather than running from it. Communicate to parents and students that you are a partner in the learning endeavor. As you raise the ceiling of expectations, you will always raise support systems accordingly.

Record Keeping in a Differentiated Classroom

When you are developing a classroom in which you differentiate content, sense-making activities, and products, it's a good idea to modify ways in which you keep track of student growth. Although teachers employ many useful strategies to chart student tasks and growth, and you likely have your favorites, it is important to remember that your methods need to accommodate assessment that (1) records student status in regard to specified learning outcomes (KUDs), (2) provides indicators of a student's habits of mind and work, (3) enables you and your students to track growth with specified learning outcomes, and (4) generates information that will not only help you plan appropriate learning experiences for given individuals and groups of students but also help students better understand how they can contribute to their own success. Guidelines presented here are meant to help you begin to develop a record-keeping system that works best for you, the nature of your classroom, and the age of your learners.

You don't have to throw out your grade book! Often, just relabeling the columns will be adequate. In a science class where all students complete a nondifferentiated and graded piece of work on a given day, the heading over the grade column would be dated and then might say, for example, "Voc. Test SS" to reflect that the grades below are for a vocabulary test on the solar system. In a class where students of varied readiness levels completed a differentiated and graded assessment on fractions, the heading might read "Fract S1D," indicating that the grades below came from the first summative assessment on fractions, and that the assessment was differentiated. A quick survey of assignments, students working with them, and dates and labels would enable you, for instance, to look at the April 9 heading and reference which assignment Jackson worked with on that day.

Use student work folders as a record-keeping device. Regardless of the age of your students, having them maintain a folder that keeps a running record of work completed, dates of completion, student or teacher comments about the work, and work samples is a powerful record-keeping aid. If you're a secondary teacher, using color-coded folders for different periods of the day can make distribution, collection, and storage easy. Student work folders, whether paper or electronic, should contain record-keeping forms (e.g., student-choice reading lists, spelling lists, skills proficiencies demonstrated, product assignments, and others), samples of student work, records of conferences with the teacher, student goals, and other data that would help both you and the student maintain a sense of focus and direction. These folders are also a powerful tool for charting student growth and visible indicators of students' work habits, and as such, they can be very valuable during conferences with students and parents. It won't take you long to discover that it's necessary to allot a few minutes every few weeks for folder clean-out. Teachers can provide guidance on what should remain in folders and what can be safely discarded.

Share as much record-keeping responsibility as possible with your students. Even very young learners can keep a calendar of daily or weekly activities, maintain records of what they are reading, record their progress at a center or station by using forms left at those workplaces, select work that they feel shows best what they have learned, and keep reflections on both positive work habits and ones needing additional attention. Students can hand out and collect folders, prepare portfolios for parent conferences, write reports or use checklists to show their progress to parents and teachers, and assume responsibility for a myriad of other procedures that make record keeping less of a demand on you. Students who serve as an "expert of the day" can often check in work, monitor accuracy of completion of tasks, or make a record of which students have worked on a given task at a given time. Helping students become effective record keepers also helps them develop clarity regarding goals, assignments, and their progress; assists them in metacognition or thinking about ways in which they can contribute to their own success and the success of the class as whole; and provides them with skills of organization that will serve them well in many settings.

Curb the inclination to grade everything a student does. Remember again that an athlete may attempt countless three-pointers during basketball practice without having a score entered in the record books. Formal "assessment" of the ballplayer's progress and skill may not come until days or weeks later in a game situation. A young musician goes to a violin lesson where the teacher explains and demonstrates what to do in order to become more proficient with the instrument. The youngster goes home to practice those skills for a week, returns for another cycle of advice and affirmation, goes home and practices again, and doesn't undergo formal assessment until a recital, weeks or months later. No one feels the need to grade each half-hour of basketball or violin practice.

A well-constructed product, performance assessment, or test should provide adequate evidence of what students know, understand, and can do at benchmark moments in a learning cycle. In between, you might make daily jottings on a clipboard you carry around during interactions with students or note in your attendance record who is or is not engaged in their work. You might record the questions students ask, points of difficulty and clarity for various students, and so forth. All this information can be used to develop assignments for students based on observed needs and strengths. By not grading everything, a teacher facilitates intellectual risk taking in students who do not have to fear making mistakes and who learn that there is an opportunity to gain a skill before they are judged. Work with colleagues and school and district leaders to adopt digital tools that help you communicate with parents about student progress. Look for tools that do not require that grades be assigned to formative learning experiences and that emphasize habits of mind and work, feedback, and progress toward goals instead of grades.

Involve students in student-led parent conferences when possible. Asking students to be a part of goal setting with you, to keep track of their work and how it demonstrates their work habits and growth, and to communicate this information to parents can be beneficial for everyone. It helps students develop responsibility for and a voice about their own work. It helps ensure that both you and the parents hear the same student messages about what's working and what isn't. It clarifies to parents why it matters so much that students have work that matches their needs. It also addresses the reality that learning itself is learned, and that students who have cooperative teacher-parent partners in finding an optimum learning match are fortunate indeed.

A Final Thought

Fourteen-year-old Kathleen wrote a poem a number of years ago. She was an advanced learner who had seldom found a serious reason to extend her academic reach in school. Then she encountered a teacher who inspired her to find new power in herself. At the end of that school year, Kathleen wrote a poem to her teacher. It really expresses the need of all students—and all humans—to push their own limits. It certainly describes Kathleen's acknowledgment of what it was like for her when that need was fulfilled. Her words also seem to express her clear sense of the role her teacher had played in that magical year, as the teacher saw Kathleen and dealt with her as an individual.

> *Push me! See how far I go!*
> *Work me 'til I drop. Then pick me up.*
> *Open a door, and then make me run to it before it closes.*
> *Teach me so that I might learn,*
> *Then let me enter the tunnel of experience alone.*
> *And when, near the end,*
> *I turn to see you beginning another's journey through the tunnel,*
> *I shall smile.*

Appendix: A Few Instructional Strategies Helpful in Academically Diverse Classrooms

Strategy: *Compacting*

Description	Rationale	Guidelines
A three-step process that (1) assesses what a student knows about upcoming content and what the student still needs to master, (2) plans for teaching what the student doesn't know and excuses student from classwork and homework in areas of mastery, and (3) plans for freed-up time to be spent with alternative assignments that may or may not be directly related to the content the class is currently studying.	• Provides a system for acknowledging and building on advanced knowledge in learners. • Eliminates boredom and lethargy resulting from unnecessary drill and practice. • Makes better use of student time once the student demonstrates mastery of required content. • Satisfies the hunger some students have to learn more about more topics than school often allows. • Encourages independence.	• Explain the process and its benefits to students and parents. • Pre-assess learner's knowledge and document findings. • Assume a student "buys out of," or is excused from, work on which he/she shows mastery to focus on more challenging work. • Allow student much choice and voice in use of time "bought" through previous mastery. • Use written plans and timelines for alternative learning. • Establish clear expectations for student work—including ways in which the student can get help when the teacher is busy. • Be sure to plan teacher interaction with the student while he/she engages with the alternative learning. • Consider using group compacting for several students when appropriate.

Strategy: *Differentiated Homework with Homework Checkers*

Description	Rationale	Guidelines
The teacher assigns students homework based on readiness so that students' work is appropriate for their current points of development with the content—or students self-select from several options based on their understanding of their own next steps. When students return to class, the teacher checks for homework completion. Students who have not completed the homework sit in a designated area of the room to complete it. The teacher works with those students while homework checker groups go over their assignments. Homework checker groups are generally composed of three or four students who did the same assignment. Students discuss everyone's answer to each question. Each student indicates on his/her paper which answers are correct and why, and which answers are incorrect and why. Students staple together all papers from their group. The teacher spot-checks one of the batch with the understanding that everyone is responsible for representing the group's decisions correctly.	• The practice of routinely assigning the same homework to all students often results in some students who have to "practice" what they've already mastered while others become frustrated or confused because they lack the skills to complete the assignment. • Differentiated homework enables students to work forward from where they are. • Using homework checkers allows for checking homework even though students have completed different assignments. • Using homework checkers engages virtually all students in discussing and explaining responses and calls on them to take responsibility for understanding and representing other students' thinking as well as their own. • Using homework checkers also gives the teacher a chance to work closely with students who are not completing homework, often because they cannot.	• Assign homework that focuses a student on practice he or she needs to move forward. • Be sure students understand the importance of practice at their levels of challenge. • Be sure students understand the process for homework checkers—including expectations for how to note justifications for "correct" and "incorrect" responses. • Teach students how to work effectively and collaboratively in groups—including homework checker groups. • Encourage students to jot down questions that arise as they check homework and to share the questions with the class or teacher as a follow-up. • Feel free to have homework checker groups review only part of the assignment, designating questions the group should address that will sample important skills and/or understandings.

Strategy: *Flexible Grouping*

Description	Rationale	Guidelines
The teacher carefully preplans grouping arrangements to ensure that students are part of many different working groups throughout a unit but also have opportunities to work alone. The teacher forms groups based on the match of the task to student readiness, interest, or approach to learning. At varied points in a unit, groups will be both heterogeneous and homogeneous in readiness level, interest, and approach to learning. Sometimes students select work groups, and sometimes teachers select them. Sometimes groups are random.	• Builds a sense of community among students. • Allows both collaborative and independent work. • Allows attention to readiness needs, interests, and approaches to learning. • Gives both students and teacher a voice in work arrangements. • Allows students to work with and learn from a wide variety of peers. • Encourages teachers to "try out" students in a variety of work settings and with a variety of tasks. • Keeps students from being "pegged" as a particular kind of learner.	• Ensure that all students have opportunities to work both with students most like themselves and with students dissimilar from themselves in readiness, interest, and approach to learning. • Assign work groups when desirable to ensure that students work with a variety of classmates. • Allow students to select groups as they are able to make good decisions about group composition that supports successful work. • Ensure that all students learn how to work cooperatively, collaboratively, and independently. • Be sure there are clear guidelines for group functioning that are taught in advance of group work and consistently reinforced. • Consider use of a few "standing" groups that are pre-assigned for a period of days or weeks.

Strategy: *Interest Centers or Interest Groups*

Description	Rationale	Guidelines
Interest centers (often used with younger learners) and interest groups (often used with older learners) can provide extension or enrichment of the curriculum by providing print and other resource materials, activities, questions, and so on that encourage students to think more broadly or more deeply about a topic than the text or standards suggest. They can also provide opportunity for students to work with topics of special interest beyond the scope of the curriculum. It's important to include materials in students' home languages whenever possible and to reflect experiences of varied cultural groups as well. Expert groups can also form around interest centers. These centers/groups can be differentiated by level of complexity and independence required, as well as by student interest, to make them accessible and appropriately challenging for all learners.	• Allows student choice. • Taps into student interest—motivating. • Satisfies curiosity—explores hows and whys. • Extends the scope of the baseline curriculum. • Can allow for study in greater breadth and depth. • Can be modified for student readiness and language needs. • Can encourage students to make connections between fields of study or between study and life. • Can be useful for anchor activities.	• Create with students expectations/criteria for successful work at the interest center or in an interest group. Fine-tune the routines and processes over time. • Build on student interests as well as interesting extensions of the curriculum. • Encourage students to help you develop interest-based tasks. • Adjust for student readiness and language. • Encourage students of like interests to work together.

Strategy: *Learning Centers/Learning Stations*

Description	Rationale	Guidelines
Learning centers or learning stations are areas of a room where students can work independently or in small groups on information, understandings, or skills (KUDs). Learning centers tend to be more permanent and to include resources that remain in the center for days or weeks. Stations tend to be more informal areas of a room designated for shorter terms and with resources that come and go from the station as student work there begins and ends. Teachers can adjust learning center and learning station tasks to address readiness, language, interest, and learning profile needs of students. Additionally, they are useful for skills and knowledge practice as well as for developing or applying big ideas.	• Allows matching task with learner's skills level or point of knowledge acquisition. • Encourages continuous development of student skills. • Allows matching task with student readiness, interest, and/or approach to learning. • Enables students to work at appropriate pace. • Allows teacher to break class into practice and direct instruction groups at a given time. • Helps develop student independence. • Can support effective student collaboration.	• Work with students to establish clear expectations for work at centers and stations and fine-tune expectations periodically. • Match tasks to learner readiness, interest, approach to learning, language, and/or independence levels. • Avoid having all learners do all work at all centers. • Make sure students know how to get help when the teacher is busy. • Monitor student understanding and progress at centers and stations. Check for understanding/ misunderstanding. • Teach students to record their own progress at centers. • Provide clear directions and criteria for success at centers and stations.

Strategy: *Tiering*

Description	Rationale	Guidelines
Tiering is a readiness-based instructional strategy. Almost any activity can be tiered (e.g., learning contracts, sense-making activities, products, rubrics, writing prompts, assessments). In planning a tiered assignment, a teacher begins by creating one version of a task that focuses students on critical knowledge, understandings, and skills, then develops additional versions of the task at different degrees of challenge. The Equalizer (see p. 85) is handy for planning tiering. It's important to begin planning for advanced students first, which is likely to make the initial lesson richer and more robust than starting at other readiness levels. Then tier by providing varied levels of scaffolding to enable most students to access high-quality learning experiences. The number of tiers to create depends largely on the readiness span in the class as determined through formative assessment. Each version of the task should be "respectful"—that is, equally interesting and engaging; each should focus students on the same essential knowledge, understandings, and skills; and each should require students to think, problem solve, support their views, and so on. The goal of tiering is to have each student working at a level of moderate challenge for that student.	• Allows students to begin learning from where they are while still working with essential knowledge, understandings, and skills. • Allows students to work with appropriately challenging tasks. • Avoids work that is anxiety-producing (too hard) or boredom-producing (too easy). • Encourages "teaching up."	• Be sure each version of the task is focused on the same essential knowledge, understandings, and skills (KUDs). • Use a variety of resource materials at differing levels of complexity and associated with different learning modes to support student success. • Adjust the task by complexity, abstractness, number of steps, concreteness, and independence to ensure appropriate challenge. The goal is not to make one version of a task "easy" and another "hard." Rather it's to find a level of task complexity such that all students will be able to complete the task with a balance of success and effort. • Be certain there are clear criteria for quality and success. • Let students know they are all working toward the same goals even though their work varies somewhat. • Follow up with whole-class discussions that enable all students to contribute.

Strategy: *Varying Questions*

Description	Rationale	Guidelines
In class discussions, in small-group instruction, in one-on-one contexts, and on tests, teachers vary the nature of questions posed to students based on readiness, interests, and approaches to learning so that all students have the opportunity to show what they know. All questions focus on the same essential knowledge, understandings, and skills, but they are posed to allow for responding in ways that align with students' readiness levels, language, experiences, preferred modes of expression, and so on.	• All students are accountable for critical content, but individuals are more likely to be engaged and experience success when questions are frequently targeted to their readiness levels, language proficiency, experiences, and interests, and when modes and conditions of response work for them. • Teachers can "try out" students with varied sorts of questions as one means of assessing progress and readiness. • Varying questions appropriately helps nurture motivation through success. • In oral settings, all students can hear and learn from a wide range of responses	• Target questions to particular students and "open the floor" to others to build on previous responses. • Use open-ended questions, or questions with more than one right answer, as often as possible. • Use wait time before taking answers. • When appropriate, give students a chance to talk with thinking partners before giving answers. • Adjust the complexity, abstractness, degree of mental leap required, time constraints, connections required between topics, and so forth, based on the strengths of the student being asked the question. • Cue questions for a student who is likely to have great difficulty answering orally because of language, shyness, etc. Let the student know in advance that you'll be asking a question and what the question will be. • Teach students—and model for them—respect for everyone's responses.

References

Altintas, E., & Ozdemir, A. S. (2015). The effect of the developed differentiation approach on the achievements of the students. *Eurasian Journal of Educational Research, 61*, 199–216. doi: 10.14689/ejer.2015.61.11

Ayers, W. (2010). *To teach: The journey of a teacher* (3rd ed.). New York: Columbia University Press.

Berger, R. (2003). *An ethic of excellence: Building a culture of craftsmanship with students*. Portsmouth, NH: Heinemann.

Bess, J. (1997). *Teaching well and liking it: Motivating faculty to teach effectivity*. Baltimore, MD: The Johns Hopkins University Press.

Black, P., & Wiliam, D. (2010). Inside the black box: Raising standards through classroom assessment. *Phi Delta Kappan, 92*(1), 81–90.

Blad, E., (2015, January 20). New milestone: Majority of public school students now considered low-income [blog post]. *Rules for Engagement*. Retrieved from http://blogs.edweek.org/edweek/rulesforengagement/2015/01/new_milestone_majority_of_public_school_students_now_considered_low-income.html

Brandt, R. (1998). *Powerful learning*. Alexandria, VA: ASCD.

Clark, B. (1992). *Growing up gifted*. New York: Macmillan.

Clarke, J. (1994). Pieces of the puzzle: The jigsaw method. In S. Sharan (Ed.), *Handbook of cooperative learning methods* (pp. 34–50). Westport, CT: The Greenwood Press.

Coffield, F., Moseley, D., Hall, E., & Ecclestone, K. (2004). *Should we be using learning styles? What research has to say to practice*. London: The Learning and Skills Research Centre.

Cohen, E., & Lotan, R. (2014). *Designing groupwork: Strategies for the heterogeneous classroom* (3rd ed.). New York: Teachers College Press.

Csikszentmihalyi, M. (1990). *Flow: The psychology of optimal experience*. New York: Harper & Row.

Dack, H., & Tomlinson, C. (2015, March). Inviting all students to learn. *Educational Leadership, 72*(6), 10–15.

Daniels, H. (2002). *Literature Circles: Voice and choice in the student-centered classroom*. York, ME: Stenhouse.

Darling-Hammond, L., & Bransford, J. (Eds.) (2007). *Preparing teachers for a changing world: What teachers should learn and be able to do*. Hoboken, NJ: John Wiley & Sons.

Deci, E. L., & Ryan, R. M. (1985). *Intrinsic motivation and self-determination in human behavior*. New York: Plenum.

Delpit, L. (1995). *Other people's children: Cultural conflict in the classroom*. New York: The New Press.

Dewey, J. (1938). *Experience and education*. New York: Macmillan.

Dweck, C. (2008). *Mindset: The new psychology of success*. New York: Ballantine.

Earl, L. (2003). *Assessment as learning*. Thousand Oaks, CA: Corwin.

Education World. (2013a, March). Creating a WebQuest: It's easier than you think. Retrieved from http://www.educationworld.com/a_tech/tech/tech011.shtml

Education World. (2013b, January). Literature Circles build excitement for books! Retrieved from http://www.educationworld.com/a_curr/curr259.shtml

Education World. (2013c, June). The "Jigsaw" technique. Retrieved from http://www.education-world.com/a_curr/strategy/strategy036.shtml

Erickson, H. (2006). *Concept-based instruction for the thinking classroom*. Thousand Oaks, CA: Corwin.

Gardner, H. (1983). *Frames of mind: The theory of multiple intelligences*. New York: Basic Books.

Gardner, H. (1993). *Multiple intelligences: The theory in practice*. New York: Basic Books.

Gay, G. (2013). *Culturally responsive teaching* (2nd ed.). New York: Teachers College Press.

Gilligan, C. (1982). *In different voice: Psychological theory and women's development*. Cambridge, MA: Harvard University Press.

Ginsburg, D. (2015, June 1). Ability grouping: Better for students or easier for schools? [blog post]. *Education Week Teacher*. Retrieved from http://blogs.edweek.org/teachers/coach_gs_teaching_tips/

Goddard, R., Tschannen-Moran, M., & Hoy, W. (2001). A multilevel examination of the distribution and effects of teacher trust in students and parents in urban elementary schools. *Elementary School Journal, 10*(1), 3–17.

Graff, L. (2014). *Absolutely almost*. New York: Philomel Books.

Grigorenko, E., & Sternberg, R. (1997). Styles of thinking, abilities, and academic performance. *Exceptional Children, 63*, 295–312.

Guskey, T., & Bailey, J. (2010). *Developing standards-based report cards*. Thousand Oaks, CA: Corwin.

Hattie, J. (2009). *Visible learning: A synthesis of over 800 meta-analyses relating to achievement*. New York: Routledge.

Hattie, J. (2012). *Visible learning for teachers: Maximizing impact on learning*. New York: Routledge.

Hayman, S. (2016, May 31). Two receive Teachers with Heart Award. *ArkansasOnline: Three Rivers Edition*. Retrieved from http://www.arkansasonline.com/news/2016/may/31/2-receive-teachers-heart-award/

Hopfenberg, W., & Levin, H. (1993). *The accelerated schools resource guide*. Hoboken, NJ: John Wiley & Sons.

Kelly, R. (2000). Working with WebQuests: Making the web accessible to students with disabilities. *Teaching Exceptional Children, 32*(6), 4–13.

Ladson-Billings, G. (1995). Toward a theory of culturally relevant pedagogy. *American Educational Research Journal, 32*(3), 465–491.

Ladson-Billings, G. (2009). *The dreamkeepers: Successful teachers of African American children*. San Francisco: John Wiley & Sons.

Lisle, A. (2006, September 6–9). *Cognitive neuroscience in education: Mapping neuro-cognitive processes and structures to learning styles. Can it be done?* Paper presented at the British Educational Research Association Annual Conference, University of Warwick, Coventry. Retrieved from http://www.leeds.ac.uk/educol/documents/157290.htm

McTighe, J., & Wiggins, G. (2013). *Essential questions: Opening doors to student understanding*. Alexandria, VA: ASCD.

Means, B., Chelemer, C., & Knapp, M. (Eds.). (1991). *Teaching advanced skills to at-risk learners: Views from research and practice*. San Francisco: Jossey-Bass.

National Research Council. (1999). *How people learn: Brain, mind, experience, and school*. Washington, DC: National Academies Press.

Noddings, N. (2005). *The challenge to care in schools: An alternative approach to education* (2nd ed.). New York: Teachers College Press.

O'Connor, K. (2009). *How to grade for learning* (3rd ed.). Thousand Oaks, CA: Corwin.

Office of Special Education & Rehabilitative Services. (2015, December). *37th annual report to Congress on the implementation of the Individuals with Disabilities Education Act: Parts b & c.* Washington, DC: U.S. Department of Education. Retrieved from http://www2.ed.gov/about/reports/annual/osep/2015/parts-b-c/37th-arc-for-idea.pdf

Olson, K., & Lawrence-Lightfoot, S. (2009). *Wounded by school: Recapturing the joy in learning and standing up to old school culture.* New York: Teachers College Press.

Ornstein, R., & Thompson, R. (1984). *The amazing brain.* Boston: Houghton Mifflin.

Paschler, H., McDaniel, M., Rohrer, D., & Bjork, R. (2010). Learning styles: Concepts and evidence. *Psychological Science in the Public Interest, 9,* 105–119.

Paterson, K. (1981). *The gates of excellence: On reading and writing books for children.* New York: Elsevier/Nelson Books.

Piaget, J. (1978). *Success and understanding.* Cambridge, MA: Harvard University Press.

Prentis, P. (2016, January). Anxiety in the classroom: Another learning disability? *AMLE Newsletter.* Retrieved from http://www.amle.org/BrowsebyTopic/WhatsNew/WNDet/TabId/270/ArtMID/888/ArticleID/579/Anxiety-in-the-Classroom%e2%80%94Another-Learning-Disability.aspx

Riener, C., & Willingham, D. (2010, September/October). The myth of learning styles. *Change.* Retrieved from http://www.changemag.org/archives/back%20issues/september-october%202010/the-myth-of-learning-full.html

Sousa, D. (2011). *How the brain learns* (4th ed.). Thousand Oaks, CA: Corwin.

Sousa, D., & Tomlinson, C. (2011). *Differentiation & the brain: How neuroscience supports the learner-friendly classroom.* Bloomington, IN: Solution Tree.

Sternberg, R. (1985). *Beyond IQ: A triarchic theory of human intelligence.* New York: Cambridge University Press.

Sternberg, R., Torff, B., & Grigorenko, E. (1998). Teaching triarchically improves student achievement. *Journal of Educational Psychology, 90,* 374–384.

Stevenson, C. (1992). *Teaching ten to fourteen year olds.* New York: Longman.

Storti, C. (1999). *Figuring foreigners out.* Yarmouth, MA: Intercultural Press.

Stronge, J. (2007). *Qualities of effective teachers* (2nd ed.). Alexandria, VA: ASCD.

Sullivan, M. (1993). A meta-analysis of experimental research studies based on the Dunn and Dunn learning styles model and its relationship to academic achievement and performance. *Dissertation Abstracts International,* 54-08A.

Tannen, D. (2013). *You just don't understand: Women & men in conversation.* New York: Harper Collins.

Tomlinson, C. (1993). Independent study: A flexible tool for encouraging personal and academic growth in middle school learners. *Middle School Journal, 25*(1), 55–59.

Tomlinson, C., & Imbeau, M. (2010). *Leading and managing a differentiated classroom.* Alexandria, VA: ASCD.

Tomlinson, C., & Moon, T. (2013). *Assessment & student success in a differentiated classroom.* Alexandria, VA: ASCD.

Vygotsky, L. (1986). *Thought and language* (A. Kozulin, Ed. & Trans.). Cambridge, MA: MIT Press. (Original work published 1934.)

Walkington, C, Milan, S., & Howell, E. (2014). What makes ideas stick? *The Mathematics Teacher, 108*(4), 272–279.

Watanabe, M. (2012). *"Heterogenius" classrooms—Behind the scenes: Detracking math & science—A look at groupwork in action.* New York: Teachers College Press.

Wiggins, G. (1998). *Educative assessment: Designing assessment to inform and improve student performance.* San Francisco: Jossey-Bass.

Wiggins, G., & McTighe, J. (2005). *Understanding by design* (Expanded 2nd ed.). Alexandria, VA: ASCD.

Wiliam, D. (2011). *Embedded formative assessment*. Bloomington, IN: Solution Tree.

Williams, K., & Williams, C. (2011). Five key ingredients for improving student motivation. *Research in Higher Education Journal, 11*. Retrieved from http://scholarsarchive.library.albany.edu/cgi/viewcontent.cgi?article=1000&context=math_fac_scholar

Willis, J. (2006). *Research-based strategies to ignite student learning*. Alexandria, VA: ASCD.

Willis, J. (2007). *Brain-friendly strategies to ignite student learning: Insights from a neurologist and classroom teacher*. Alexandria, VA: ASCD.

Wolfe, P. (2010). *Brain matters: Translating research into classroom practice* (2nd ed.). Alexandria, VA: ASCD.

Index

The letter *f* following a page number denotes a figure.

About the Author

Carol Ann Tomlinson began her career in education as a public school teacher, and she spent 21 years as a classroom teacher and in administrative roles. During that time, she taught high school, preschool, and middle school students in the content areas of English/language arts, history, and German. She also served as the district director of programs for advanced and struggling learners and as school community relations coordinator. While a teacher in the Fauquier County (Virginia) Public Schools, she received recognition as Outstanding Teacher at Warrenton Junior High School, Jaycees Outstanding Young Educator, American Legion Outstanding Educator, and Soroptimist Distinguished Women in Education Award. She was named Virginia's Teacher of the Year in 1974.

Tomlinson is currently William Clay Parrish Jr. Professor and Chair of Educational Leadership, Foundations, and Policy at the University of Virginia's Curry School of Education, where she is also co-director of the university's Institutes on Academic Diversity. She works with both graduate and undergraduate students, particularly in the areas of curriculum and differentiated instruction. She was named Outstanding Professor at Curry in 2004 and received an All-University Teaching Award in 2008. In 2017, *Education Week*'s Edu-Scholar Public Influence Rankings placed Tomlinson 13th on its list of the United States' most influential higher education faculty members in terms of shaping dialogue about education and 4th in the field of educational psychology.

Tomlinson is the author of more than 300 books, book chapters, articles, and other educational materials including (for ASCD) *The Differentiated Classroom: Responding to the Needs of All Learners* (2nd edition), *Fulfilling the Promise of the Differentiated Classroom: Strategies and Tools for Responsive Teaching, Differentiating Instruction and Understanding by Design: Connecting Content and Kids* (with Jay McTighe), *The Differentiated School: Making Revolutionary Changes in Teaching and Learning* (with Kay Brimijoin and

Lane Narvaez), *Leading and Managing a Differentiated Classroom* (with Marcia Imbeau), and *Leading for Differentiation: Growing Teachers Who Grow Kids* (with Michael Murphy). Her ASCD books have been translated into 13 languages.

She works regularly throughout the United States and internationally with educators who seek to create classrooms that are more effective with academically diverse student populations. She can be reached at Curry School of Education, P.O. Box 400277, Charlottesville, VA 22904 or by e-mail at cat3y@virginia.edu or www.differentiationcentral.com.

Related ASCD Resources: Differentiated Instruction

At the time of publication, the following ASCD resources were available (ASCD stock numbers appear in parentheses). For up-to-date information about ASCD resources, go to www.ascd.org. You can search the complete archives of *Educational Leadership* at www.ascd.org/el.

ASCD Edge Group
Exchange ideas and connect with other educators interested in differentiated instruction, multiple intelligences, and the Whole Child at the social networking site ASCD EDge® at http://ascdedge.ascd.org.

Online Courses
Differentiated Instruction: An Introduction (2nd ed.) (#PD11OC115M)
Differentiated Instruction: Creating an Environment That Supports Learning (#PD11OC118M)
Differentiated Instruction: The Curriculum Connection ((#PD11OC116M)
Differentiated Instruction: Teaching with Student Differences in Mind (#PD11OC138M)

Print Products
Assessment and Student Success in a Differentiated Classroom by Carol Ann Tomlinson and Tonya R. Moon (#108028)

The Differentiated Classroom: Responding to the Needs of All Learners (2nd ed.) by Carol Ann Tomlinson (#108029)

Differentiation in Middle and High School: Strategies to Engage All Learners by Kristina J. Doubet and Jessica A. Hockett (#115008)

Differentiation in Practice: A Resource Guide for Differentiating Curriculum, Grades K–5 by Carol Ann Tomlinson and Caroline Cunningham Eidson (#102294)

Differentiation in Practice: A Resource Guide for Differentiating Curriculum, Grades 5–9 by Carol Ann Tomlinson and Caroline Cunningham Eidson (#102293)

Differentiation in Practice: A Resource Guide for Differentiating Curriculum, Grades 9–12 by Carol Ann Tomlinson and Cindy A. Strickland (#104140)

Integrated Differentiated Instruction and Understanding by Design: Connecting Content and Kids by Carol Ann Tomlinson and Jay McTighe (#105004)

Leading and Managing a Differentiated Classroom by Carol Ann Tomlinson and Marcia B. Imbeau (#108011)

"What Differentiation Is and Is Not" (Poster) (#115068)

Video
The Differentiated Classroom: Responding to the Needs of All Learners (DVD Series) (#615049)
The Power of Formative Assessment to Advance Learning (3 DVD Set and User Guide) (#608066)

For more information: send e-mail to member@ascd.org; call 1-800-933-2723 or 703-578-9600, press 2; send a fax to 703-575-5400; or write to Information Services, ASCD, 1703 N. Beauregard St., Alexandria, VA 22311-1714 USA.